BOOTS:
AN
UNVARNISHED
MEMOIR OF
VIETNAM

Stephen L. Park

BOOTS: An Unvarnished Memoir of Vietnam

by Stephen L. Park

Published by Writers AMuse Me Publishing, August 2012 (British Columbia/Boston/Los Angeles)

ISBN: 978-1-927044-43-8
ISBN10: 192704443X

:

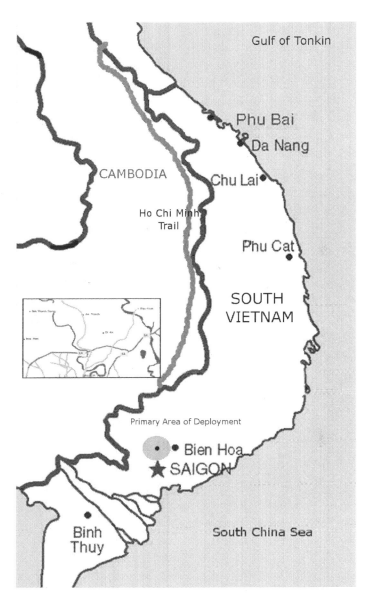

Gulf of Tonkin

Phu Bai

Da Nang

CAMBODIA

Chu Lai

Ho Chi Minh
Trail

Phu Cat

SOUTH
VIETNAM

Primary Area of Deployment

Bien Hoa

SAIGON

Binh
Thuy

South China Sea

PRIMARY AREA OF OPERATIONS

Stephen L. Park

DEDICATION

*This is dedicated to my wife Sherry, who equally endured,
my daughter Jennifer, who questioned, and to the families of
the men of Delta Company who gave their lives.*

.

ACKNOWLEDGMENTS

A special thanks to Mary, and Dave, whose encouragement and unlimited assistance kept me going.

.

1

I was at 35,000 feet. War was looming on my mind. Knowing someone on the same flight had not been foremost in my thoughts. Seeing that it was Lieutenant Ed Mello was not a bonus. Mello, a former classmate in the Infantry School at Fort Benning, Georgia, was a likeable, fast-talking, street-smart kind of guy from Boston. He always flashed a big, white-toothed smile while talking some kind of shit. It had been a mistake to rent him my car.

A few weeks before our graduation, I had bought a new car, a 1967 Chevy Camaro, but kept my old 62 VW Beetle rather than trade it in. It sat unused in a parking lot near our barrack and when Mello found out, he asked if he could rent it.

He had met a woman in town and wanted a quick way to get back and forth from base during our sparse free time. Her husband was in Vietnam. I didn't share his idea of good fortune in finding a woman, but as a favor to him, I agreed to whatever he offered to pay. It wasn't much, but when it came time to pay, it was always 'I'll pay you later'. We lived by an honor code, but it only went so far with him. He never paid. I never forgot the lesson learned. It was nothing like the many lessons I would learn in the year to come.

#

My orders arrived in October, 1967. I was assigned to the 1st Infantry Division, known as the Big Red One; the shoulder patch was an olive green background with a large, embroidered red one in the center.

In February1968, Mello and I jumped off a truck at the 90th Replacement Company at Long Binh, Vietnam where we waited to be picked up by another truck that would take us to our base camp. There I was, in a real war zone for less than an hour, already checked in at our transit headquarters, when Mello says, "Hey Park, I'm going to shoot some pool. Come get me when we're ready to leave." He was off to find a pool table. I didn't bother to respond. It was inconceivable that anybody's first priority in a war zone could be to play pool.

There were about a half-dozen of us going to the First Division. A clerk wielding a clipboard with the manifest list announced, "Transportation will be here soon, so don't wander off."

There was no sign of a war going on during my first hour on the ground. The 90th was a gathering place of incoming and outgoing personnel jumbled together, yet easily recognized as two distinct groups: The outbound, mostly tanned and looking relaxed; the inbound showing the February paleness of the stateside winter. It was a place without real activities, soldiers in limbo, going one direction or the other, names on lists waiting to be called. Purgatory for some, it was a perfect time and place to move around, ask questions, glean any useful information. The ultimate goal was learned quickly: be back here in twelve months as a member of the outbound group.

As told, the truck was there within the hour, and every man was onboard except Mello.

The driver yelled, "Truck to the 1st Division is leaving!" His words relayed through the company area.

Mello came running, breathless and climbed on, "Why didn't you come and get me?" He was indignant.

"I didn't know where you were," I told him. True, I didn't know, but it didn't matter. I owed him no favors and would have left his ass there to catch the next truck.

#

As the truck rolled toward our base camp in DiAn, Mello resumed his usual style of constant chatter. He had already planned his return to the states, a long year away.

"You know what I'm going do when I get back to the states? After I land in San Francisco, I'm going to Seattle, buy an Austin Healey and drive back to Boston. I'm going to drive back home, cross-country."

It was a good enough idea, something that could be done by a single man, which he was. I thought, 'Personally, I wouldn't be able to get across country quick enough.' A year was a long, long way off.

We were assigned to the same battalion but different companies. Once dropped off in my new company area, I never saw him again; he didn't return to the 90th Replacement Company or drive cross-country in an Austin Healey. Lieutenant Mello was killed in action less than three months later. I was sorry to get word when it came through the grapevine. War never cared about the future.

2

War was a disappointment. It was that simple. I sat around battalion headquarters two or three days, read our operations manual and listened to random radio chatter that meant nothing to me. I made friends with clerks and talked in my sleep, evidence offered by the battalion doctor who repeated my nocturnal rambling. I slept on a ceramic tile floor in a small room along with another eight or ten men.

#

The morning dawned for me to meet my platoon. I grabbed my gear, ready to venture into the boonies. It turned out that the platoon was only a two- or three-mile jeep ride away, another disappointment. Delta Company was set up at a new, modern water filtration plant on the edge of Thu Duc, a large town a few miles northeast of Saigon.

The plant was as contemporary as any stateside installation. Inside were showers and toilets, and in my impatience for war, I would fail to appreciate those luxuries. I recently left those small things taken for granted, but I wouldn't see such comforts again until R&R six months later. My indoctrination was too safe; I was anxious to see the war, to live the stories I had listened to since my induction.

My arrival was not the only thing happening in the company at that point. The place seemed to be turning upside down. I was introduced to Lieutenant Mel Brav, third rifle platoon leader; it was called November platoon. Instead of numbers, all platoons used phonetic alphabet names: Lima and Mike were the first and second rifle platoons and Oscar, the fourth, was the weapons platoon - three 81mm mortars. I was Lieutenant Brav's replacement.

"Grab your gear and come on," he said. It was my first full official act in war as far as I was concerned. "I'll take you to your bunker."

Even the thought 'I have my own bunker?' was exciting at the moment. I tried to not look too wild-eyed.

Lieutenant Brav's time was up to rotate out of the field to become the new company Executive Officer (XO), a base camp job assignment. He was big and burly, black hair, heavy black-rimmed glasses, and wore what I thought was a permanent scowl on his face. Periods of humor were short, as his own life there was in turbulence, between my arrival and the captain leaving. In his defense, I soon realized a full-time scowl wasn't an unusual facial expression for anyone in the field.

There was no need for more than a quick introduction to Captain Carden, the company CO. He was also packed up, leaving the field for a new assignment. It was a busy day. As soon as he left, Lieutenant Brav would be acting CO until a new one arrived. I didn't know that at the moment, but it could have explained Brav's mood.

#

Out front of the water plant, a new four-lane highway passed connecting Saigon to the right, Bien Hoa to the left. Heavy traffic on the highway was another bit of unpleasantness as far as I was concerned.

Providing protection for the water plant from saboteur's attacks was a critical assignment. It had been attacked during the Tet Offensive a few weeks earlier. My new company had been dispatched to Saigon during the major Tet battles in Saigon, and the men were content with the security assignment. For them, it meant short daily patrols, sitting around in the heat and dust, playing cards under makeshift shade.

\#

Captain Shaw, my new company commander, rolled in two or three days after me. I hadn't anticipated an inexperienced CO, one less experienced than myself. He smiled all the time and looked like a rosy-cheeked mama's boy who didn't get much sun; I chalked it up to fair skin. He was knock-kneed – impossible not to notice – and gave the impression he needed corrective boots even when he stood still. His entire look appeared effeminate; odd for a grunt, I reckoned. I imagined he would be uncomfortable beating the bush walking like that. There was nothing about him that said he belonged in the field.

He reminded me of an unpleasantness I had in completing the Jungle Operation School in the Panama Canal Zone two weeks before I left for Vietnam. We were broken down into four-man teams for an Escape and Evasion exercise; our team leader was a Captain who sat behind a desk in Germany the three previous years. Unable to read and understand a map, he insisted we could walk around a swamp. It was an impossibly foolish idea. We wasted so much needed time that we got caught in dangerous rock-ledge mountainous areas with sheer drop-offs, late in the night. Fifteen hours later, we were the last team to finish the course.

There was nothing about my new CO that instilled confidence in me.

\#

The initial two weeks in county felt like a period of acclimation with a distinct lack of danger. We patrolled the minimally populated landscapes around the outer edges of town and once or twice, parts of the town itself. I generally amused myself by observing aspects of the new culture where I found myself.

On patrols through town, it was impossible to follow the straight-line compass directions we were given; we were passing through an abstract maze of city streets and alleys. We zigzagged our way.

On one of the more memorable days, we walked down an unusually narrow alley edged by a row of crudely constructed buildings. A lone teenage boy stood ahead of us, carrying a large, bulky box fastened on each side by a strap worn around his neck. Instant alert; I knew the stories about kids carrying booby-traps to detonate in groups soldiers. Our approach from behind slowed to a stop.

I walked up to him to check the box, giving it a good once over, looking for trip switches or wires. He opened the top. The box was insulated and partially filled with frozen treats on sticks. The kid was their version of the neighborhood popsicle man.

One tiny kid suddenly sprang out from behind a loose board in the side of a building. Without a word of common language, he managed to get a free treat with my compliments. The vendor was happy to take our military currency script, not a problem to use on the Black Market - money was money. That single purchase sent out a signal. In a matter of seconds, we were swarmed by a half-dozen chattering kids jumping around. Donations were taken from the platoon until each one had received something to eat before they ran away. I wondered if any of them would remember the event when they were old men - the day that American soldiers bought them treats. It was a good day of war.

3

It was my second week in the war, and I had not fired a round for any reason, but neither had anyone else in the company. Time was quiet and boring, aside from nearly getting shot in the head one afternoon. The platoon was just in off patrol, and I tossed my gear on the bunker. A round whizzed by my head as I stood beside my bunker chugging a cold Pepsi, a top priority when returning from the heat. I was on the ground against a low concrete wall in a split second.

"Jesus, where the fuck did that come from? What kind of dumb son-of-a-bitch is doing that?" I couldn't believe it - the thought of dying while drinking a Pepsi. My learning curve had started.

I never heard a weapon fire, but South Vietnamese military units trained in the area and were the main suspects.

#

Each of the three rifle platoons left on their patrols, staggered by two-hour departure times, and each patrol was four hours. My platoon had completed a morning turn and was back inside our company NDP (Night Defensive Position) at the water plant by noon.

The other part of our daily mission was to act as a reinforcement force if needed. In mid-afternoon we got the call: "Saddle up. Tanks and APCs (Armored Personnel Carriers) will pick you up on the south side of the perimeter."

The second platoon, Mike, was out on afternoon patrol when they got into a fire fight three or four kilometers away. The place was called 'the factories'. It was no more than a couple of deserted two-story, rectangular white stucco boxes accented with broken windows, remote, except for a close-by small farming village. My men said it was a good place for VC contact. Going there was like going to a good fishing hole.

On top or our armored transportation, we roared down the Saigon-Bien Hoa highway at full speed before turning left onto a cross-country route. It was a five-minute ride.

Our armor rolled up, and the entire village of forty or fifty people ran from their one-room, stick and palm frond hooches. It looked like they knew something I didn't know about what was about to happen. They rushed straight toward us in mass evacuation, some carrying their possessions on their backs. From their point of view, we were a bad sign, and no doubt better to come toward us than run away and be mistaken as Viet Cong. They knew war and fear, and that it was not good for us to be there.

I was hoping for what had seemed like long-awaited action. By the time we arrived however, it was over, a body count of one. I had never seen a VC, but there he lay in the dirt, full of bullet holes. He looked like other young Vietnamese men, wearing only the ubiquitous black shorts and no shirt. He had been shot by every man in Mike platoon, perhaps as some kind of unity within their platoon, or simply as a message to other VC... or for the hell of it. I didn't ask why. It was just the kind of shit grunts did; hardcore stuff. His dust-covered body was left to be recovered by those who knew him. Death received little dignity.

The two platoons milled around a few minutes. Our newly-arrived company commander, who rode down with us, told the other platoon to load up. With space for only one platoon to ride, I thought 'What the fuck is he talking about?'

Hell, they had covered less than half of their patrol route, while we had done all of ours, plus gone to help them out. For us to walk back was the same as telling us to do another patrol. Even Lieutenant Moore, Mike platoon leader, was surprised but he wasn't about to refuse their good fortune.

"Why do they get to ride back?" I asked the captain. "We have already done our full patrol today."

"Because they had a body count," he said, wearing the shit-eating grin he always did.

"A body count?"

They killed one fucking VC and they got a ride back and the rest of the day off? That was the typical, arbitrary decision-making technique he used with regularity. It may have seemed like a small point. It wasn't. Morale was a fragile thing and you didn't screw over people in the field.

My radio operator stood beside me. Only one thing could come out of my mouth. "Can you believe that son-of-a-bitch?"

It was the first step of our new captain's decline of respect within the company; he never recovered.

4

IIot damn, we were briefed for an air assault the next day! That was the best briefing yet in my short war life. Air assaults - the stories I'd heard since Basic Training made me feel like I was really in the war, or at least a special part of it. LZs (Landing Zones) and PZs (Pickup Zones) were the stuff of legends, dangerous stuff if you received ground fire either coming or going. The air assault was something I had been hoping for, waiting on. I was pumped. But there was a valuable lesson in it for me, unexpected certainly and not taught at the Infantry School.

Three platoons stood in the large area outside the concertina wire in the front of the water plant, waiting on the Huey's. Often called a "Slick", the Huey was a workhorse of a chopper and was the only form of transportation we used for air assaults. They traveled in flights of five, small groups capable of carrying a single platoon. That morning it was the same five choppers pulling shuttle duty, dropping off a platoon and returning to pick up another; occasionally there were fifteen at a time if the entire company was traveling a long distance.

Each platoon was broken down into five separate groups of five or six men. Each load group stood by to run toward the open doors on touchdown; seconds later they were in the air again. We weren't the first platoon out that morning and that was fine with me; it was my first time and I didn't want the insertion and security at the LZ.

When they returned for us, I was the last man in our group to climb in. I wanted to have the best perspective possible from the air as I sat in the doorway, cross-legged. I was determined to have the outside space on the floor.

The Huey rose a few feet, the nose dropped as we lifted forward on the rise, climbing quickly in altitude before banking to make a one-hundred-and-eighty degree change of direction. For some un-thought-out reason, I expected them to go more vertical and stay flatter when they changed directions. There had never been much reason to think about the ride itself.

Halfway through the turn at about two hundred feet altitude, I looked almost straight in front of me and saw nothing but the ground.

'I am about to fall out of this fucking thing and die right here.' It was my thought. I was truly scared.

If the floor had been smooth and slick it would have happened as I could feel my weight shift toward the door, only the fabric seat of my pants gripping the checker-plate floor. The twenty-five or thirty pounds on my back would assist in a faster fall.

I didn't believe, or at least hoped, that none of my men could see the flash of sheer panic on my face as my left hand shot straight out beside me to grab the door edge, straight-armed, pushing back for all I was worth. Nothing could be reached on the right side.

In the military, there is always the ten-percent factor. The ten-percent are the ones who didn't get the word, didn't hear, got lost - the non-thinking screw-ups not in sync with whatever was going on with the rest of the world. It was part of my job to always watch for the ten-percent guys.

After the chopper incident, I hated like hell to believe I had been the ten-percent factor that morning; the idiot. War had no place for stupidity.

5

"Pack up. We're moving."

Without advance notice, word came mid-day. My pulse made an up-tick at the thought of change. I felt like I was finally getting a fresh start for the war. None of the men were familiar with the location. It would be a new area that the whole company would see together for the first time. Our movements worked the same every time thereafter, never a notice.

Flights of Hueys appeared in the distance, small dots without sound – fifteen of them; three flights of five were spaced seconds apart. The first five hardly set down before a half-dozen soldiers quickly scrambled on board with field gear and rucksacks, everything they owned. The choppers lifted off just as quickly, and five more came in seconds behind them, then the last group. The company was airborne.

I sat within handhold reach of the door frame that time, but still kept my doorway position on the floor, with an unobstructed view of everything below us.

Flying time was short, maybe five minutes, when I caught sight of bunkers below. The distance of the move wasn't so great, but in terms of visual change, it could have been a thousand miles. There was no traffic, not so much as a motor scooter, no roads, no buildings, nothing.

From the chopper, the NDP was geometrically laid out in a circle maybe a hundred meters in diameter. On a large flat, treeless field the olive drab humps of bunkers spaced about ten meters apart were the only prominent features.

The choppers dropped and settled on their skids a few meters outside the stacked rows of coiled concertina wire forming the perimeter of our new home. Looking around, there was nothing but dirt and a few tufts of dead grass. Blinding dust swirled in the air from the choppers' rotor wash. It was a solitary looking place with severe, solemn accommodations. The contrast with the water plant more closely matched my expectations before arrival in country.

#

Although drafted, I was glad to be there, in a perverse way. War had its own strange lure, and I accepted the fate of my role long before arrival. I trained for it, bought into the idea of war, with a surplus of youthful naiveté to be perhaps overly curious about war. I was twenty years old and still possessed the feeling of innate immortality, but the false bravado of group roars, growls, and chants repetitiously performed in training was gone.

Changes within myself were to come quickly, subtly, almost tangible within the next two weeks. I could feel it inside as I changed from sentimental ideals to the cheap reality of war, the 'learning curve where a year of aging could be done in a month' type of shit. It was something no amount of training could duplicate. It was part of becoming hardcore.

#

The company in the NDP had been there the previous two weeks and was prepared for their exit. Some of the men in my platoon were moving around, asking questions as I had at 90th

Replacement, gathering intelligence about the area based on the other company's experience.

Frequent enemy contact had kept them busy. Their last patrol brought in two Viet Cong POWs and a small weapons cache, including a heavy machine gun. I hoped we would be so lucky. Their own battalion intelligence section reported the possibility of three hundred VC in the area; we had no reports although in the future it was not unusual to receive such intelligence.

This was at least a semi-permanent installation. Bunkers were already dug, there were no sandbags to fill; that was a welcome work saver.

My platoon secured a third of the perimeter as did each of the other two rifle platoons. The fourth platoon was a weapons platoon. They worked and lived in a central part of the NDP with the mission of providing fire support if needed by patrols or ambushes.

Each perimeter position was a three-man foxhole, chest deep with a roof and walls on the front and both sides several sandbags high. Two firing ports were built into the front. Behind the bunker was a low rectangular wall, three sandbags high, enclosing about fifty square feet. Inside the enclosure, three men slept, stored rucksacks, ate, and escaped the fucking merciless sun under low roofs fabricated from our dark green, plastic ponchos; we were lucky if our heads cleared the roof while sitting underneath.

We settled into our assigned positions, exchanged our old maps for ones of our new area of operations, and received the daily briefing for the next morning's patrol. My platoon had point, and I had a plan.

Dusk lapsed into dark as helicopter gunships worked an area to our north; another unit was in a firefight. Artillery flares kept a constant glow with the downward swinging on their parachutes. I turned my back; the distant illumination provided enough light over my shoulder to scribble a quick letter home.

6

We saddled up, ready to move out at 0800. 'Shit, it's going to be a hot one' I thought. It was hot before we started.

The previous evening I briefed our platoon sergeant and squad leaders on the patrol. They marked their maps with compass azimuths, checkpoints, and distances; everything I knew about the next day, they knew.

My daily order was that squad leaders brief every man in their squads so the whole platoon would know exactly how far, which direction, and what terrain to expect on patrol. I often walked around spot-checking, asking men at random what we were doing the next day. I believed that maximum information kept down questions, relieved anxiety, and let each man make his own mental preparations.

#

"Move out. Lock and load." Bolts were pulled back then released, snapping a round into the chamber as each walked through the wire. Inside the NDP our procedures were to leave the chamber empty; it avoided accidental discharges.

Patrol length was only three kilometers that day; I was pumped up. I knew that with us on point I would have us back by noon, eating our C-ration lunch sitting in the NDP. I had studied the map closely after our briefing, and I had no doubt. Three Ks, almost two miles; my mind twirled at the thought. 'Shit, I can't believe somebody screwed up on our patrol distance, thinking it would take more than four hours to move three klicks."

Before we could clear the concertina wire gate, sweat beads rolled down inside my shirt, already wet under the straps of my gear. Five-meter spacing between men was taken up as we moved out. Small clouds of dust rose no higher than boot tops. The only sounds were those of gear being shifted to find a comfort level.

One detail of my plan for a short day never entered my mind: the possibility I could be totally wrong. I was. It took ten hours to cover three thousand meters, two hours longer than a usual patrol day.

Our route started through old rice paddies, which were dormant and dry, partially overrun by grass and scrub brush. Beyond those, the day was wet and shitty.

In depths of anywhere between our knees to our waists, we waded through brackish water that remained even through the dry season. That was the good part. Beneath the water was sandy mud; every step became a battle with a boot-sucking beast that would ooze to the top of the laces, clutching the boot, not wanting to relinquish its hold. Further back along the formation it was even worse, as the men had to walk in mud fully softened and stirred by those at the front of the line

Rest breaks were taken hourly for a breather or the chance to slide some gear off my shoulders for a few minutes, but relief was sparse. Without shade and often no place to sit, standing in the sun was of questionable benefit. The five or ten minute break per hour plus another thirty minutes for a C-ration lunch added more than hour to the day.

I looked back during one break and saw our company commander, who had been out on two patrols since his arrival; both had been air assaults. He was clearly standing in a state of misery, without his usual shit-eating grin. The sight put a smile on my face. I was still new, but I paid my dues for two weeks of patrols and knew what the heat felt like. I thought, 'Welcome to the field, shit-head.'

Enemy contact for the day consisted of two VC bodies found, one partially buried, one in a small pond of water. The cause of their deaths was unknown. Nobody got close enough to investigate. We kept walking, and I wondered if they were destined to have their bones eventually sink into the mud, never to be found.

#

Two weeks before Vietnam, I was enrolled in the Army's Jungle Operations School in the Panama Canal Zone. One of our tests was the earlier-mentioned Escape and Evasion course.

Our start point was on the edge of a swamp; swamps were indicated on maps by small blue marks representing an undefined area. Two of us knew how to read topographical maps. The Captain who was to be our leader did not. The dumb-ass thought we could walk around the swamp if we traveled past the blue marks on the map. The Sergeant and I finally convinced him that the marks were symbolic only, not defining, but we had wasted over thirty minutes trying to walk around it before he waded through water that ranged from waist to chest deep.

I was twenty feet away from a bank when I heard a quick thrash of weeds and a large splash from my left. I never looked, but leaned forward in the gut-deep water, moving as quickly as I could push my legs. There was no doubt to me it was a Caiman, the Central American version of an alligator, deciding to take a closer look, but that is a different story. The lesson was that water markings on maps were never a predictable reality; they were easily changed by rain or wet seasons, or drought conditions.

#

Maps of our operating area were veined with thin blue lines; water symbols. It was generally a crap shoot as to what they would look like upon arrival, especially in the dry season. Some streams were a walk-through, and some required a rope and swimmer. We had both types that day. One man stripped his gear at the wider, deeper crossings and swam across to tie the rope, allowing passage for the remainder of the patrol.

Flowing water felt good, no matter how hot or dirty, but I always thought of what may lie upstream. I was leery of everything and imagined the worst, a rotting corpse or a shallow crossing that was full of water buffalo shit. Whatever was in the water washed around my submerged cans of C's, and the tops of my canteens of water I would be drinking from all day.

The extra weight of waterlogged gear, boots, and uniforms was offset by the cooling effect it temporarily provided. It was a time-consuming operation by itself to move two platoons across a thirty-foot span. One-by-one, men slid down one muddy bank, did the slow hand-over-hand pull with both arms stretched above their head, lucky if their shoulders were above water, and climbed up a bank that was made even muddier by the traffic.

#

I didn't see the events but heard the report about the rear platoon's crossing. They managed to lose the following: one steel pot, one 40mm grenade launcher, one AN/PRC-25 backpack platoon radio, and amazingly, a shirt. I never understood how some dumbass could lose a shirt, but it set a stupidity record that was not surpassed the duration of my time. It was one of those days the problems for that platoon far exceeded the ten-percent factor of fuck-ups. My personal joy was that my platoon had no part in the fiasco.

7

The environment – in the forms of heat, tedium, muck, and more – was an enemy in its own right, and was a constant battle for each man. Some aspects were uncontrollable; other personal discomforts were lessened through either trial and error or compromise.

I was in good physical condition, but the first day in that NDP had my ass dragging. I hadn't prepared for a ten-hour patrol. I dropped my gear on my last step to the bunker, wanting two things: drinkable liquid and mail.

Within minutes, I was bloated after gulping unlimited amounts of hot water too fast, but there was no mail. Mail from home was, without doubt, the most important thing in the field, but delivery was always delayed until supplies were redirected to our new NDP.

Without a letter to read several times over, I had the time and the need to start thinking my daily routines: water, the fit of weighted straps across my neck and shoulders, socks – simple shit I hadn't bothered to think about before. Small annoyances grew into major importance as the day progressed, and one day's discomfort was amplified by its continuation on the next day. There was no such thing as comfort, however effort was made to avoid the aggravation of general discomfort. Nobody in the platoon complained about the common misery we shared; everybody carried the gear.

The third item on my list was to remove boots and wet, muddy socks so my feet could dry after eight hours of wetness. Socks were quick to become a major issue. I had one pair. At first I let them dry and put them back on but the dried, stiffened sandy mud was equal to putting on coarse sandpaper. The only solution was to wash and dry them first each day, and a daily laundry ritual was not an immediate desire upon return every day.

On one patrol, I skipped the socks completely. They were going to be wet and muddy anyway, and it would save the step of washing when we got back. It was a fucking catastrophe. At every rest stop, I removed my boots to beat and dump the sandy grit from inside. The wet sand in the mud stuck to the wet insides of the boots and made life miserable. I loosened laces, tightened laces – nothing helped the rawness caused by the coarse, grinding silt of each step.

I sent word by way of the supply chopper to send me another pair of socks. Soon, a clean, dry pair waited for me at the NDP every day as I washed out the pair I had worn. They were the only thing I had in the order of extras, and clean, soft, dry socks were probably second only to mail so far as comfort returning from patrol.

#

We were on a training exercise for several days in the worst parts of Fort Benning, Georgia. With an intentional lack of supplies, I drank swamp water collected in waterproof sleeping bag covers and treated with purification tablets. It caused a constant headache for two days and had to be strained through my front teeth while drinking, to keep the trash out, but its taste was no worse than the drinking water in Vietnam.

Nothing about our drinking water there quenched thirst. Whatever the source, it had no refreshing quality; it was wet and that was all. It came to us in either five-gallon Jerry cans or in a small trailer-mounted tank air-lifted in by supply choppers. The taste was made worse by the plastic canteens and ambient temperatures in the nineties. It had a taste that made me want another in two minutes, when the feel of a mouth full of cotton balls came back.

I talked to others in the platoon about water consumption and found part of the problem was to take the first drink too early in the morning. It became an informal competition to see who could last the longest each morning. My two quarts were gone by the hottest time of the afternoon, but I learned better. It was a terrible punishment to be parched, unable to spit, the last hour or two in the dehydrating afternoon heat and humidity. When canteens were emptied, water was substituted by one or two salt tablets rolling around in the mouth for minimal moisture until they became unbearable and were spit out.

Like the sock problem, I picked up another canteen and set a goal of 1100 hours before the first drink, but they were still empty when I set foot inside the wire each day. I refused to go with four canteens and have to carry eight and a-half pounds of water every day.

8

A rarity, we had three straight days of air assaults. They put us in areas which expanded our physical presence in the boonies, well beyond our normal patrolling range. The job was the same once we hit the ground, but flying – having a ride to and from work – provided a psychological boost. It also took time as we sat waiting on the choppers, setting up LZs and PZs. It was time spent not walking, favoring our work hours considerably.

The only point of trepidation was the possibility of a hot LZ, receiving fire on arrival. It was on my mind each time we were first in, but it never happened to me, and I was thankful. A hot LZ was bad news. Huey door gunners or escort gunships often used recon fire into the areas around the LZ. It was always without warning, enough to momentarily scare the shit out of anybody.

Choppers never actually landed, but momentarily held a low hover above the water while we exited. I would look at my dry pants and boots as we descended the last few feet, then below, at the water and force myself to make the jump into waiting muck.

"Shit, I hate jumping in this fucking stuff."

A few days later we jumped into knee deep mud and water. Dry ground was less than fifty feet to our right where we could have been dropped with equal ease. I was convinced that son-of a-bitch pilot put us over the paddy on purpose. It was the only water we touched all day.

#

The first day we were the drag – the rear formation – for two platoons. Our mission was to patrol a section along the Dong Nai River that bordered our division's area of operations. It was a large river that merged with the Saigon River downstream. It was on the map but hidden from our view by a screen of vegetation that grew uniquely along its banks. Moving straight from the LZ, it looked more welcoming from a distance than up close. The point man entered, slipped a few meters inside the swath of growth and turned right. The river was no more than a few meters on our left flank, but was never seen through the dense forest of stalks.

I was glad to be there. The vegetation was something I had only seen distantly from choppers and my platoon didn't have point which meant we were on a sightseeing tour. The rear platoon did no more than provide a reserve force for the lead platoon. We moved single file due to conditions.

The men called it Nepa Palm, but it wasn't. That was just the name passed down to identify the plants for our own use. They weren't palms at all. Since there were no botanists in our platoon, the name was good enough for us. I don't think they were even trees. The fifteen-foot high plants had multiple smooth green stalks sprouted from one huge base; they shared physical features of the Elephant Ear plants growing wild along Florida canals and in Southern yards, except for the unusual tree-like height. Large as the big end of a baseball bat, the stalks were immovable and thick growing as they crisscrossed upwards toward the green leafy tops.

Hardly a shard of sunlight reached down through the solid green canopy. Nothing grew beneath. The river bank was dark umber mud, hard packed, damp, its surface both slippery and gummy when disturbed by our intruding boots.

It was the type of terrain benefitting the Viet Cong; thick foliage provided concealment from the air and allowed natural following of the river toward Saigon. It was a torturous trek through the thickest parts, stepping sideways, squeezing my way through unyielding stalks, gear and weapons hanging up at every opportunity.

#

In early afternoon the lead platoon found two bunkers constructed of the near black riverbank mud, the perfect camouflage that made them invisible from only a few meters. Each one was made of three walls and a roof. They were vacant upon our arrival, but were actively used as a medical aid station and place to eat, as supplies showed. Among the items were an unexploded 105mm. artillery round and a duck, sitting calmly with one leg leashed by a light cord.

The find was called into battalion headquarters.

Unexpected luxury time struck while we waited for the battalion commander to fly out two forty- pound shape charges, fuses, and detonation cord. As last in line that day, my platoon had the honors of setting the explosives while the point platoon moved out two or three hundred meters.

"Anybody here know how to set these charges?"

"Yes sir, I know how to do it." Sergeant Rayborn assured me he was capable of setting and wiring the charges.

I was slightly skeptical because it meant he was smarter than I had given him credit, and I made sure I wasn't too close to him while he worked with the det cord and fuses. A ten-minute timed fuse was lit, and we made our way sluggishly across a deceptively marshy weed patch, checking our watches, not wanting to be too close.

It was a hell of a sight. Massive chunks of mud, looking to be the size of a Volkswagen Beetle, and vegetation blew right through the canopy. Debris must have flown straight up twenty feet. It was one of those "Holy shit" moments, followed by laughter at the obvious overkill in the explosives department; it was fun to have something to laugh about on a miserable patrol day. The mud rejoined its original state, and we felt bad about the duck, but there was no reprieve, no day to take prisoners. We only accelerated its ultimate fate while denying the VC a meal.

The fireworks ate away time until it ended the day's patrol, and we moved directly on to our PZ; there were no complaints about the shortened day.

The rule for air assaults was, last in-last out. That was us, last. The other platoon shuttled back to the NDP on the first flight while we waited for the five choppers to return. For our extraction procedure, claymore mines were set pointing outward, nearly encircling the landing zone in the style of porcupine quills. With remote detonators in hand, they were blown as we rose from cover and ran to the arriving choppers.

#

Hot, tired, and muddy, lying back waiting on the PZ, every pair of ears listened for the familiar sound of the Hueys in the distance. It was practically a competition for who had the best ears and heard them first, yelling an enthusiastic 'choppers', best suited for a Bingo parlor. The sound of the Huey was undeniably distinctive - whap, whap, whap, thump, thump, thump sound of the rotors as power was eased off and on. Nothing else sounded as sweet or was more dearly appreciated as the volume increased.

In less than a half-dozen air assaults, I was an experienced chopper rider, quick to learn to sit closer to the door edge, one hand to hold on in case of any sharp movements. I had advanced to find the most useful part of the ride home was dangling my legs from the doorway, pants flapping in the wind; they always dried before landing and boots partially dried. I always had the whole doorway to myself, never understanding why some of the men wanted to sit on the canvas bench seat that ran from side to side.

#

That evening, the news of the day was a firefight by Bravo, a sister company, at the factories near the Thu Duc water plant, the same place our 2nd platoon had made contact a week or so earlier. The men were right when they told me the factories were a good place for enemy contact. Bravo had two casualties, both were platoon leaders; one dead, one wounded.

Bad situations and outcomes served as academic discussions, as close as grunts had, about the affected unit.

"It sounds like Bravo doesn't have their shit together."

"Yeah, they stepped on their dicks today."

"I'm glad I'm not in that company."

And so it went, as if Bravo Company had some jinx or a curse, and we could ward it off by our speculation of their shortcomings. We wanted to believe it couldn't or wouldn't happen to us. It was necessary to confirm our confidence that we would never be caught without our shit together; we were too good of a unit. In less than two months, it would happen to us – with worse results.

9

It was our morning for point. Three or four kilometers and two checkpoints later, the company walked single file, parallel with the river. On our left flank, a large, dry rice paddy, on our right, the same type of nearly impassable, aggravating riverbank vegetation we encountered on patrol a couple of days earlier.

We were moving between natural cover of tall grass and saplings which had taken root at the edge of the paddy, and the mass of green stalks. My kilo, the radio operator, and I were up close to the front, appreciating the surprising ease of movement and dry conditions of the day.

Specialist4 Ware walked five meters ahead of me. He was a good man from Mississippi, and to call him unexcitable was an understatement. Passing by a small opening in the grass on our left, he half-stopped, and turned to speak.

"There's some VC out there in the paddy to our left front," he said as nonchalantly as he possibly could.

I couldn't see for the vegetation, and in the lowest voice I could scream, "Jesus Christ, turn around and fire! What the fuck are you telling me for?"

It was hard believe our point man didn't see them, but I guessed he would have to look in the right direction at the right time as he passed by the hole in our cover.

Ware opened fire at the same time the men in front caught sight of them and started firing. Seven or eight VC were quick to scramble over a dike, less than a hundred meters ahead. I never saw them; I was busy on the radio the second it started.

I finished quickly describing the situation on the radio to the CO., and brought the next squad behind me up to our left flank. The captain ordered us to use fire and cover tactics, where one squad fired as the other ran forward a few meters, then reversed roles, leap-frogging forward to the end dike where the VC disappeared. We weren't receiving any fire. I thought the whole process too slow, exposing men in an open paddy instead of the lead squad moving forward under cover.

The VC had long since vanished into the grass and scrub brush beyond the paddy. The back side of the dike was laid out with individual nesting spots lined with large leaves and grass. Some of the men speculated they may have been lying in wait to ambush us, but they wouldn't have had enough advanced notice of our arrival, and it wouldn't have been the most advantageous position either. I suspected they either slept there or were spending the day, waiting. Our patrol was going the general direction of their escape, but we weren't going into a chase mode in the thick cover.

#

It was close to lunch time before we got organized and moving up front. The way things worked during contact, the platoon in the rear was in basic standby in case we needed them. They were probably digging into their C-rations, or taking a break, listening to reports on their radios, since they were neither involved nor going anywhere. Unlikely to be moved forward, they had nothing else to do. That was the nature of close-in contact. There was only so much space, usually for no more than a handful of men.

Regrouped and ready to move on, one of the men spotted a couple of VC behind him, at one of the river mud bunkers. I was probably fifty meters back from the front men when they dropped for cover and started firing. I saw a narrow opening going toward the river. Thinking it was maybe an old path cut back through the dense growth, I made a run for it to possibly find better angle on the bunker.

A second later, Sergeant Rayborn jumped up, running behind me. "You shouldn't be going in there by yourself, Lieutenant. Let me go first."

I thought that was rather nice of him; the sergeant being the one who set the explosives in the riverbank bunkers blown to hell earlier. His concern raised my opinion of him considerably.

"Okay, let's see if we can see anything in here," I said.

It was nothing more than a false path, promptly ending in a matter of feet. We stopped and crouched down, peering into that fucking green wall of stalks, unable to see anything, when the bastards opened fire on us. I didn't know where the first rounds went, but we dropped as flat as road kill. Rayborn and I had enough space to lay stretched across the narrow opening, but not much more and no place to go.

Peeking up, I finally saw muzzle flashes from the low, black, igloo-like mud bunker. It was hardly visible through the crisscrossed growth, not more than fifty to seventy-five feet away; it was hard to see more than ten feet. They had a firing port two or three feet above ground level, where there was better clearance to fire. Our heads were against the thick bases that sprouted the clumps of stalks. In front of us was nothing but a wall of the green. Even if we could've gotten our rifles above ground level, there was zero field of fire; rounds couldn't travel three feet without slamming into vegetation.

Fortunately, the same obstacles that prevented us firing also protected us. Some of the bullets that made their way through were zinging stalks directly above our heads, but couldn't get to our level. They could definitely see us. I lay, hoping the stalks weren't hard enough to allow ricochets; otherwise there was no sense of danger, much like games played as kids. The best plan was to lay there, face in the mud and hope my helmet was made of good steel, just in case.

I was yelling information about what and where we could see, to my kilo, still under cover by the rice paddy. He forwarded the messages to our CO.

Battalion headquarters, monitoring our company's radio frequency, already had a gunship on the way. At the sound of a chopper a few minutes later, we popped colored smoke grenades marking our position, for safety. The men at the front of the platoon threw a red smoke as far as they could over the canopy, toward the bunker; red smoke indicated enemy positions only - never friendly locations. The smoke grenades and sound of the helicopter caused the firing to stop. Rayborn and I crawled out.

The whole platoon pulled back to give the gun ship clear space. The chopper was the new Cobra, and it was the first time I had seen one work up close. It was a terror for close-in air support, carrying an arsenal of a 20mm. nose cannon, pods of 2.75 inch rockets on either side, and a 7.62mm minigun. The chosen weapons were pairs of rockets fired in sequence.

Not quite far enough away, one of my men was hit in the mouth by a piece of flying shrapnel and received two broken teeth. Thankfully he was not in immediate pain so there was no need to call a Medevac chopper.

The Cobra finished its work. My platoon swept the river bank area - nothing. An empty bunker and footprints headed toward the water were all we found. That was the result of four hours work. I was soaked by sweat, face in the mud, and the place was infested with fucking red ants, the angriest, meanest, and largest ants I ever saw. They were half to three-fourths of an inch long, the color of boiled lobster. Pincers on their head were used to hold their bodies straight out, applying full force during their attack. Necks were the preferred body part.

It was a disappointing day, the score: zero to zero. We abandoned the remaining patrol route and reversed our morning direction to return; the rear platoon became the lead.

In the morning, we had walked around the edge of a small village of maybe a dozen hooches. Returning, we walked through the center. Our company interpreter, Charlie Mi, was walking along with me when he became curiously suspicious about something none of us would have noticed. He and I stopped to look closer.

10

I didn't know Charlie Mi except to say hello around the company area. He was shorter than typical Vietnamese, and his face, the color of cured tobacco, made him look older than he was, although I guessed he was in his mid-thirties. I doubted he'd ever spent a day inside, away from the subtropical sun. Deep brown, shiny hair matched his complexion and a big, friendly, warm smile made every man in the company his friend, and vice-versa.

Somewhere he had a wife and kids, but his full-time home was in the field with our company. We were standing around one day when he said, "Lieutenant, I can show you the way the police in New York taught me to fire a pistol. You do it this way and use two hands." He spread his feet, bent his knees, held both arms straight out with hands together as he fired an imaginary pistol from his sturdy stance. "Never use one hand," he said, "always two."

Charlie had gone to New York City to train with the police department and was proud of it, but nobody carried a pistol in the field. It was against our procedures; not even medics carried pistols. At one time, they were worn by officers and soon became primary identification targets of the enemy.

He normally traveled along with the company commander, but returning that afternoon we walked together in the rear. As we walked through the village, he noticed an old man cooking, or maybe it was the size of the cooking pot that caught his eye.

"Lieutenant, let's go and see what he is doing."

I radioed ahead for the company to hold up while we took a look. The small village lacked any sign of prosperity. I hadn't seen any fields being worked by villagers, and nobody else appeared around the hooches except for the old man, stirring the oversize pot over an open fire. Small and wrinkled, with long, stringy, silver-gray hair, he slowly worked a large wooden paddle.

The steady steam from the black iron caldron that hung by chains from a tripod reminded me of winter hog killing when I was small. Charlie bent over the huge pot to look. I did the same out of curiosity, not knowing what to expect. A dozen or more packets, the size of bricks, wrapped in green leaves and tied, were being stirred around. Suspicious, Charlie asked in a normal voice, why he was cooking so much food. The old man said it was for children coming from another village. Translating to me as he spoke, Charlie didn't believe the old man. The pot stirrer never looked up as Charlie and I spoke in English. I wasn't totally familiar with the area but couldn't recall any nearby villages. I always looked for such places from above while we were on air assaults, and no others showed up on my map.

Charlie kept asking, his voice getting louder each time he received the same answer. Within the minute, he was screaming at the top of his lungs, shaking his fists at the old man. I would've never imagined Charlie in such a rage, and thought he was about to beat the shit out of that old man. My own eyes were no doubt big by then from the surprise, but I wasn't going to stop the tirade, certain he knew what he was doing. Charlie told me "it is too much food for children".

Things did not add up, and the more logical answer was that it was food for the local Viet Cong, possibly the ones we encountered near the river.

Our captain, who had not an ounce of curiosity about military matters, didn't bother to walk back to find out about the story. He finally called back on the radio.

"November 6, this is Delta 6. Let's move out."

The day was over, for all practical purposes. It was time to move on. Charlie and I believed we walked away from a potential source of intelligence. I would have at least made a search of the few hooches there, maybe even called battalion and requested a mission change. We didn't have our claymore mines with us for ambush but could have circled around out of sight and kept an eye on the village that night.

Had we stayed for awhile longer, maybe looked around the village, who knows what we would have discovered. Something was happening; somebody was going to get a fresh-cooked meal. It was also impossible to know whether the villagers were cooperating with VC, or were being forced by way of threats.

#

It was routine to get up the next morning and not think anything about the previous day. It wasn't the case with the four hours spent the day before, chasing around for nothing. I had finally gotten to where I could taste the war, and it wasn't as I expected. Except for the initial excitement, it was a waste and I was certain there was something to be learned about poor execution and missed opportunity. The VC were maybe thinking the exact same.

My platoon had a short patrol that morning. We left the extra weight of surplus water and C-rations behind, saving about five pounds, and moved quickly. Back by 11:30, still fresh and dry, we had beaten the building heat. We also had ambush for that night.

The afternoon off was filled by cleaning all weapons and ammo that had been repeatedly submerged in muddy water and coated with dirt. Most of the platoon stripped off their shirts, rolled pants legs to above the knees, and found a tolerable spot to sit to strip every round of ammo from magazines to clean, dry and reload. Each man carried about three hundred and fifty rounds.

Sitting out in the sun on our little circle of dirt was about like sitting on the front burner on a stove, or maybe inside the oven; after the four hour job was finished, white body parts became pink, then red. I don't believe anyone thought about sunburn when we started. There was no Noxzema cream for sunburn relief either.

Whether it was good timing or a good omen, we would be glad to have everything clean, but would pay for the burnt shoulders and knees.

11

I had a calendar that fitted my billfold. A picture of Jesus was on the front with 'Follow Me' at the bottom. Our uniform shoulder patch at the Infantry School at Fort Benning also had 'Follow Me' embroidered across the top; I considered it a good luck coincidence, a 'Jesus in the infantry' kind of joke. The calendar was marked with twenty-one Xs. Days of the week were all the same, all nameless, no weekends, but an X represented a day closer to home. Twenty-one were certainly nothing to brag about, but seven more and a month was gone. After three weeks, I had reached a reasonable level of comfort with the platoon; I thought they knew they could trust me to keep them out of trouble if at all possible.

The night before, I put an X across March 17 on my calendar.

I hadn't had a bath in a week, the same as everybody, and lost my comb the week earlier, so I couldn't comb my hair which hadn't been cut in over a month. The supply chopper left a large pile of clean clothes every three or four days; it was one big pile of pants and shirts for the company. If there was nothing left that would fit, and that was likely if I was late at the pile, I kept wearing what I had. There was no comfort wearing oversized clothes, and fresh ones would be as dirty as the old ones within twenty-four hours. I still washed socks every day.

The first few nights we lived under an early full moon that rose low on the horizon as darkness came. Since we had zero use of artificial light in the field, its illumination was put to maximum use, extending letter-writing time in the NDP to well past the usual 1945 hours darkness. The moonlight became less and appeared later.

#

Briefing for that night's two-platoon-size ambush was done, coordinates marked, layout of our platoon's position studied, weapons and ammo were cleaned. My platoon had responsibility to set up a kill zone. Lima, the first platoon, would provide rear security. I didn't know where the captain would be.

We took point for the twenty minute walk, a kilometer and a half south of our NDP, and arrived about 1930 hours, past dusk, not quite dark. The company stopped nearby while we did a quick recon of the exact positions. Ambush sites were never set up until right at dark, in case we were watched; that was part of our division's operating procedures. We waited for a little more darkness before moving in.

The site was a T intersection of two dirt and grass cart paths six to eight feet wide. The primary path was straight and flat with a huge open field on the side opposite us. To our left, the path went to the village where the old man stirred the large pot of food. The other direction, I had no idea, but later found out it led to a blown-out bridge spanning a small river. We walked down the intersecting path starting near our NDP.

One corner of the intersection had four or five abandoned, deteriorating one-room stick and grass hooches ten to fifteen feet wide. About the same amount of space was between them. Their front doors lined the edge of the cart road. We lay in a line behind the hooches. The other platoon formed lines behind us, completing a triangular formation, and faced the opposite direction which was tall grass.

Immediately after dark, the platoons silently moved into their positions and began setting out claymore mines in front of the hooches. The claymore mine was an antipersonnel weapon that sat at ground level with bipods stuck in the ground. It weighed three and a half pounds, filled with plastic explosive and small steel balls embedded in a hard resin. If they were available, the men borrowed extra ones from the platoon staying in the NDP. My platoon set out fifty to sixty of them.

The platoon was broken down into three man positions, spaced with more experienced men at each end of the line. The two ends were critical; they were the positions likely to trigger an ambush. I was near the center with my radio operator and platoon medic. Our position was in one of the openings at the rear corner of a hooch.

Adding to the pain of the sunburn, somebody sent out a load of flak jackets to wear for ambush, and everybody was cursing the heavy, cumbersome relics. I was sure they were artifacts from WWII bombers.

"It may stop shrapnel, but I bet if we laid it out here and shot it, a bullet would go right through - it wouldn't stop shit," one of the men said; it was a consensus opinion. "They weren't worth shit to us."

They may have been good in some places, or for REMF's to grab on the way to a bunker, but to us it was more deadweight to haul. REMF was a slang acronym, pronounced remff – a Rear Echelon Mother Fucker; basically anyone who slept inside the wire of major fortifications or base camps. Predetermined as useless, the vests were the first thing to come off at arrival, helping to cover the prickly stuff we had to lie on for the night, not to mention relieving sunburned shoulders

Each man went about his business of preparations without speaking or noise. Everyone was finished and in position by 2030 hours. I hadn't settled for two minutes when noises began. In the distance were voices and the metallic jingle of rifle slings. In a few seconds, I realized the sounds were heard from first one direction, then another. The talking was loud and constant as the two groups stopped to meet directly in front of the hooches.

Specialist4 Dave Palmer, from Michigan, was our point man on patrols and anchored the right end of our line. He opened fire with his M-14 rifle... or rather he tried to open fire. After one round his rifle jammed. He yelled "Fire!" His ammo magazine had a dent, found the next morning, and jammed the spring that pushed up the rounds; he was screwed on that. Lucky for him it was unneeded.

Remote detonators for the claymores were already in hands; the second after Palmer screamed, explosions began. The claymores, no further than twenty feet in front of us, required a back-blast minimum safety distance of fifty feet. The lack of safe distance was compensated by tilting them up slightly to deflect the back blast to the ground. I don't know if they were all tilted or not; a cloud of debris - grass, dirt, grit, anything that was on the ground – billowed up in the air and flew through us. I took cover from our own trap. Erratic exploding thunder filled the night. There was no worry about reaction from the front of the claymores.

Before our platoon's claymores completely stopped, one man on the rear security blew his, which set off the whole platoon into doing the same.

Startled, I swiveled around to look, thinking 'What the fuck are they doing, there are no VC back there.'

I thought they were wasting claymores we may yet need that night. Soon, I knew it had to be a matter of adrenal reaction; not knowing for sure what was going on, they took no chances. By the time it was over, we had been encircled by seventy to eighty claymore detonations. It was a hell of a lot of noise, more than I'd ever heard and closer than I'd ever been.

A quick finale, the enemy never fired a shot and wouldn't have known for more than a split second what had happened to them. They stood less than ten feet in front of the barrage of claymores that continued to explode after they fell to the ground.

The claymores were heard by the weapons platoon leader back at our NDP. Without waiting on radio communication, he readied illumination and high explosive rounds for the three 81mm mortar tubes. Unlike artillery or tanks that loaded ammunition at the back end of the barrel, mortar rounds dropped down the top of a tube by hand.

He told me the next morning, after we returned to the NDP, "I could hear the explosions and got ready. I had the rounds laid by the tubes and men were standing by to drop as soon as I got the call on the radio."

I asked, "You mean you could hear us, back here?"

"Shit, you wouldn't believe how we could hear you. It sounded like Hell was going on out there. I wondered when it was going to stop."

The mortar flares started firing constantly, producing an eerie light as the round small parachutes swung in the blackness. With three mortar tubes, at the same time, they were sending out high explosive rounds in a wide sheath about a hundred meters, or two, beyond our positions. The high explosive rounds saturated the surrounding area in case a larger VC unit was close to our ambush position.

The mortar platoon behind us, fired overhead to their targets. I prayed for no short rounds, hoping all firing charges were good and no gunner miscounted the number to get down range.

Battalion headquarters, monitoring our radios, acted immediately. In less than five minutes, gunships arrived, strafing the area with rockets and spraying with rapid fire guns to supplement our mortar fire.

I did a verbal check, passed down our line of positions, to see if everybody was okay, but we lay motionless and quiet, still listening. We didn't know if anybody else was out there, maybe out of range of our claymores. I wasn't sure what to do next, not completely convinced it was over, but didn't see any reason to do anything. We had no way to know if it was a squad we hit, or if it was the point for a large enemy unit close behind them. I was content to let the mortars and gunships go as long as they wanted, while I collected my wits.

One of the VC did not die immediately and from the direction of the sound, I thought he was in front of the hootch beside our position. Without knowing if the moans were unconscious reflexes of the body, or of true conscious pain, it seemed more humane to toss a grenade to end the inevitable. It failed, but I was unsure of where else he could be. I was unable to throw any further to my left because of the building. Several minutes later, he stopped. It ended a night of one-sided war.

12

My heart was still pounding fast, my brain working to reassemble. "Hot damn!" I was unsure if there had been some kind of radio communication with the captain. I didn't want to hear from him. We must have talked. He called again to order, "Go out and sweep the kill zone."

I didn't respond, but relayed the message around me. The men were waiting on some kind of communication. Squad radios in the platoon also heard the order and helped spread the word.

"What is he talking about: 'Sweep the kill zone!' That son of a bitch is crazy - fuck him!" That was the unanimous sentiment, mine included.

I'd enough of the dumb-ass's arbitrary, hair-brained decision-making the last three weeks. The vision I had of sweeping the kill zone had the possibility of some bad things happening. I couldn't imagine anything good happening by us going out into the flare-lit open ground. Our own mortar flares had been supplemented by 105mm artillery flares that burned brighter and fell slower. The play between light and shadow had an ominous, surreal effect.

I didn't want to go and stand under that much light. The dead men a few feet in front of us damned sure weren't going anywhere. I wanted to lay low for a little while, let the platoon catch its breath and make sure nothing was moving anywhere. We didn't have much for cover, but we did have the advantage of concealment as long as we didn't give our positions away.

The order came again. He made sure I knew it came from battalion; impatient bastards sitting nice and comfy by their radio. I passed the word. On "go" the platoon got up and rushed in mass the kill zone out front of their individual positions. There was no formation or order. They wanted a sweep, we gave the fuckers a sweep, a fifteen second sweep.

My foot hit the edge of the kill zone and stopped as my eyes surveyed the area end to end. I was nearly sick. Frozen in a moment of panic, all I could see were green fatigues that looked like ARVN's, South Vietnamese soldiers. They were all carrying U.S. military rifles. I was expecting to see black clothes and AK-47 rifles. There were no AK-47's, normally used by Viet Cong, in sight. I had a queasy feeling that we had killed a group of ARVN's.

All weapons and loose items were grabbed from the distorted bodies, unsightly by the flarelight. Some heads were hit by a second claymore after falling to the ground.

I was back on the radio as soon as I could get to it, "I think these are ARVN's. They're all wearing fatigues and carrying our weapons."

A different kind of quiet hung over the platoon while the message went to battalion headquarters and in turn to the Vietnamese District Headquarters in Thu Duc. Several minutes passed before it was it was verified that no ARVN's were operating in our area; I took a breath of relief but wasn't one-hundred percent sure even with their assurance.

We settled down and maintained our position for the night; the dead, a few feet away, maintained theirs. At first light, the captain wanted to sweep the kill zone himself, to no one's surprise; he could have gone ten hours earlier with us, but things looked different then. He didn't want to participate then.

#

The captain's radio operator was called Dude. Everybody liked him. He had sandy hair and a constant squint from the sun that made him look like he was always smiling; half the time he was smiling anyway. He was in my platoon when I arrived, but moved to one of the CO.'s radios; it was a promotion for him, safer than carrying a platoon radio. All of his friends were in my platoon so we always got first word about anything newsworthy going on in company headquarters.

Later that day, back in the NDP, one of the men asked Dude, "What was the captain doing while the claymores were blowing?"

He laughed. "I don't know. All I could see was the radio line sticking out from under his helmet. He was trying to get his whole body inside his helmet I think"

That brought out a roll of disdainful, appreciative laughter from the men.

13

In first light, a body count of eight lay on the cart road. Any loose items missed the night before were gathered, the remains left to be recovered by either the VC or locals; both would have heard the nocturnal hell and known the results.

Returning from a river bank patrol days later, we found another body. We walked point and found him a few hundred meters from the ambush location by following the stench in the air. He either escaped from the edge of the kill zone with a mortal injury, or maybe escaped un-injured, only to fall to the mortars or gunships.

Lying in the full heat of the sun and bloated to twice a normal size, there was no chance of recovery by his friends. When the imperceptible breeze shifted directly towards us, I retched at the awful, rotted smell. My mind switched to a time my father and I walked upon a dead, bloated cow on our farm. I was about eight. He walked to the house and returned with his axe to cut and shape a small sapling into a spear while I gathered dead underbrush. With the spear plunged into its side to relieve the pressure, we covered the cow with brush and set it on fire. I thought it was an honorable funeral for the cow. The dead VC would have been so lucky, but that was war for you. He was left to rot.

#

Recovered weapons from the ambush were: two .30 caliber carbines, two M-16 rifles, one CAR-15 rifle, and a Colt .45 caliber pistol. Two .32 caliber Chicom (Chinese communist) pistols were the only two weapons that weren't American. I would have liked to have known the origins of the M-16's and especially the CAR-15 rifle, a newer, compact version of the M-16, not even available to us in the field. I believed it would have been issued to Special Forces teams, military advisors with Vietnamese units, or other specialized unit; it was far from a commonly issued weapon.

Other items recovered: five hundred 7.62mm AK-47 rifle rounds, twelve RPG (rocket propelled grenade) rounds, fifty dollars worth of local currency, a black hammock and a document pouch full of papers. I received the hammock and twenty-five dollars worth of currency; all the documents were sent to battalion and brigade intelligence sections to decipher. Containing intelligence about the local VC organization, the papers created a flurry of excitement. Higher-ups were buzzing; the battalion commander flew out for a firsthand account of the ambush, talking to men individually.

"Medals will be awarded." That's exactly what he said.

'What in the hell for?' That's exactly what I thought.

He was only the start; the assistant division commander was on the way, only to get side-tracked by a firefight up north.

#

The brigade's intelligence section decided to fly out and photograph the bodies the next morning, hoping to learn their identities. Some were no longer identifiable due to the full power of claymores. My platoon was scheduled to provide security, but the CO changed it to the first platoon instead; it was typical of his decision-making.

They flew into a hot LZ, receiving ground fire. It was hard for me to believe the VC would venture that far in the open in an attempt to recover the bodies; it may have indicated the importance of their casualties. It was a command group we killed. They lost five more lives from combined efforts of the platoon and the gunships escorting the brigade team. They didn't get the photos.

#

The brass was doing a good job of making us proud. I had no idea we had done anything extraordinary. It was the perfect execution of an ambush like the 2nd Brigade had never seen, maybe the whole damn division. Shit, we were practically famous in local military celebrity.

Not only did I not understand the why of the sudden uproar, it was amusing as I viewed it both as participant and curious observer. My main thought was that it vindicated our previous day's four hour long chase for nothing. I was glad to finally be involved in a positive action, as well as happy for the platoon for the same reasons. It had been a boring spell for them since Tet.

We had done what we were supposed to do. It was nothing outside my expectations, nothing considered special. It was a simple game where two teams tried to kill each other. My only surprise was that it didn't happen more often; I fully expected such actions to be a regular occurrence.

I didn't share the elation of higher headquarters. We didn't share the same perspective of events. Unable to understand why they would consider awards for doing our job, maybe I didn't understand the Army, but we enjoyed the day off.

The next morning before 0800, an anonymous message sounded over the company's radios: "Delta, Delta be advised, a Texas longhorn is in the skies."

That was the code for our division commander's helicopter. Major General Ware had a longhorn's head stenciled in black on the nose of his Huey. The radio message meant look alive. To have a two-star general walk into our NDP anytime was a shock, much less at that time of day. Division headquarters was probably forty to fifty miles away. I couldn't help but gawk.

His mission was to award about a half dozen medals in a simple field ceremony. Side-stepping from one man to the next, pinning on medals, there was no pat on the back, or smile, or sense of friendliness on his face; he was a man I could understand and appreciate.

Job done, his waiting chopper lifted off, rose a few hundred feet when the engine stopped.

I was watching him leave. "Oh, shit."

His pilot perfectly performed the technique of auto-rotate, letting the rotors spin freely without power, creating a fast glide back on our flat, open field. The chopper skidded in, its nose rocking forward as it came to the full stop. Another chopper appeared and ferried them out within minutes; later a Chinook flew in, hooked his Huey up and hauled it away.

The morning amusements were over by 0930. We saddled up, headed back to search another area of river bank. We found one black-mud bunker containing medical supplies and disposed of it with explosives in a less spectacular show than days earlier; each sector patrolled along the river turned up active bunkers, some we destroyed, some not.

#

I learned General Ware's military history after his death eight months later. His chopper was shot down, killing everyone aboard. Drafted in WWII, he was awarded the

Congressional Medal of Honor for action during the Battle of the Bulge at Bastogne, and was the only draftee to reach the rank of Major General (two stars).

#

The story of the ambush ended many years later, at a high school class reunion in the mid-eighties.

My old friend Ray and I were sitting outside talking about nothing in particular, when he said, "You're famous, you know."

"And you're full of shit. What are you talking about?"

"Yeah, you did an ambush that they're teaching in the Infantry School at Fort Benning."

"No shit? You've gotta be kidding me. They are teaching my ambush at Benning? I wonder where in hell they came up with that."

"I don't know, but they are."

"Kiss my ass. I'll bet they're not teaching how damn scared we were."

Ray had been drafted a few weeks after I had, and took the same path through OCS (Officer Candidate School) at Fort Benning, GA., ending up as a grunt in Pleiku. We talked some more about nothing in particular and later went and smoked a joint.

14

With the first platoon replacing us on the day's escort mission, the battalion commander was not around, and the assistant division commander's trip cancelled, we had an unheard of day off. It was the first one with neither patrol nor ambush.

The day was a perfect time to reflect, question, or absorb more of the learning curve I had faced. A jumble was going on in my head at the time, searching for comprehension of the previous twenty-four hours from every aspect.

'Blood.' I was thinking that morning as I stood there at daybreak, 'Why is there no fucking blood?' That was the part that surprised me; I pictured myself in their place and thought, 'If I was laying there, I think I would have bled.'

Higher commanders acted as if we had performed our mission with perfect clarity and control, 'perfect execution' they would say. They never knew what luck meant, how it controlled life in the field. Nobody asked Palmer about control, or his thoughts when his rifle jammed after firing one round. They failed to ask men about mental clarity during the thirty seconds of breath holding, praying, cursing and hoping all at the same time, waiting for things to stop. They returned to their beds when the radios returned to silence; time for a good night's sleep.

We shared a mutual goal with the Viet Cong, just opposite perspectives. I realized I had no personal animosity toward them, nor respect, which was an error because enemies always deserve respect. At best it was indifference, making them objects of prey; it was the kind of thinking that helped keep you alive. Sergeant Dennis, one of the squad leaders, did hate them twenty-four hours a day, and was willing to kill civilians he thought might be the enemy. I learned to keep an eye on him; he was a good squad leader, but I thought his ability to kill too quickly made his character less so.

I believed there were two of us in each man, the outside that performed our job, and somewhere inside was a normal human being, watching.

There was also the invisible curtain of rank that kept me at arm's length from becoming one of the men, unable to participate in their complete levels of camaraderie. Neither was there any bond with the other platoon leaders, each fully immersed in their own unit. I had, in fact, a lonely job.

That day off, the whole platoon took on a transformation, a unity of spirit not seen before. The men were happy, talking, comparing their details of the havoc created on the ambush. It wasn't normal conversation, but more about death and survival, speaking in a hyper state of primeval pride. I could imagine similar ancient ceremonies, jumping around a slain woolly mammoth with spears in hand, leaping in celebration of success on life's battlefield. The mammoth hunt mutated through the ages into war.

Usual moral values regarding death were suspended, supplanted by dehumanization and preference for the crudest, vilest language, the most derogatory terminology directed at our enemy. Normal values would have to be found anew once war was left behind. Attitudes of indifference were both a necessity and a by-product of our job, a grunt's job. 'Hardcore' was a mojo believed to ward off bad things; it was worn inside the head.

The day's spirits were singular to our own small tribe, not shared with other members of the company or higher commands. Late in the day, the euphoric state of the men was tempered by a case of the 'shakes' as some of the men called it, quietly sitting when that evening's darkness found them. Calm returned. It was something not taught at Fort Benning or any other place. Classes were on preparation and execution of a plan but not what to do afterward, of what to think or how to act.

Death was assigned as impersonal and valueless for the men lying on the cart road, but I later came around to think about their families, not in the same sense as I would for our soldiers, but families on both sides shared a neutral world, subject to sorrow. Like us, the men were young, but they were not likely to have any kind of family funeral. Maybe their remains would be unknown forever. Would the soldiers have left photographs for their memory? Would their families be proud of their deaths, fighting for a cause? Were they married? Fortunately, I didn't have to think about American families that night. There were no casualties on our side. For the families of my men, it was just an ordinary day.

15

Our first day back on patrol after the ambush was almost as if it never happened. The high point of the day amounted to the discovery of a small cache of processed rice, about seventy-five pounds. The excitement amounted to the same as finding an active bunker, good for a couple hours of interest, but nobody could shoot rice. Still, it was better than nothing; the consolation came in the destruction of several hundred meals for the Viet Cong. We hoped they went hungry.

Boredom was a constant in the field. Walking all day or lying out all night without results got old quickly. The ambush offered a temporary reprieve, but boredom always waited nearby. It was a manic-depressive way of life, up and down mental states between hyper vigilance and tiredness; mail and thoughts of home were the best daily reminder to look to the future. The prevention of reckless complacency was aided by the fact that we changed locations every two weeks. It prevented us from becoming too accustomed to our surroundings and losing our mental sharpness.

#

Morale was a disease that, if bad, was worse than boredom and could plummet for the slightest reasons. We always walked a keen edge of keeping focused on our job, to not get sloppy or distracted. A negative distraction could come from anywhere. When it came to assignment briefings, the company commander's unpredictable decisions were usually the reason for poor morale; every man expected a fairness of order when it came to patrol and ambush duty.

I went to an evening briefing at the company CP. "November platoon, you'll have a platoon size patrol tomorrow; you also have a twelve-man ambush tomorrow night," was the bottom line given by the captain. He changed the order of rotation we used daily, and the fact that we were supposed to be off the next day was not his concern.

A day off simply meant no patrol because we would have ambush that night. It was an exchange of the day shift for the night shift. The schedule we operated by was two days patrol, one ambush, each of the three platoons equality of missions. Each day two platoons patrolled while one stayed in the NDP to provide security and rest for ambush.

The platoon was anticipating the next day off. I knew what was coming before I briefed the platoon; there was no shortage of comments as the whole platoon soon found out the next day's operations. "Goddamn it, Lieutenant, that's not right. We're getting fucked on this deal. This sucks, why the fuck do we have patrol plus ambush tomorrow night? Why do those other fucking platoons get off?"

The sentiments were the same for every man including me, except I had no one to hear my complaint. I didn't have any answer other than to say that was what we would be doing. Since the schedule came from the captain, he was the target of the verbal hostility. Any bridge of loyalty we had to him was long since burned.

We were seriously low on manpower, down to under thirty men in the platoon. Twelve men were the size of one squad at full strength. As we were, it was effectively half the platoon if we subtracted me, my kilo, and the medic. On the return from patrol, half the men would need to prepare mentally and physically change some gear to go back out for the night. The remainder were spread thin to fill the whole platoon's defensive positions in the NDP. It meant little sleep for anyone.

#

Low morale shouldn't be confused with normal everyday complaints. It was the nature of grunts to grumble. I considered it a universal fact that a happy soldier was a complaining soldier. It was the object and intensity of the complaining that mattered. The standard items were things like C-rations, patrol conditions, ambush locations, and anything unnecessary.

We had a world class complainer in the platoon by the name of Broos. Unquestionably competent, his contemptuous attitude toward his lowly station in life at the time could be read by the way he stood. With thirty-five pounds of gear strapped on and hanging off, he still managed to maintain the look of bored aloofness, like a petulant teenage girl; his California origin was superior in coolness and reason to anyone else in the field. I believe he felt he shouldn't have been there like the rest of us.

At platoon briefings or meetings with the sergeants, Broos stood just close enough to eavesdrop. It allowed him to form a verdict of a plan's intellect before attending a briefing by his squad leader with the rest of the men.

He could've been the platoon philosopher, except for the narrowness of his message. He had only one philosophy: "The bigger they get, the dumber they get," referring to command rank and their ideas. He never once heard a good plan, some just worse than others. Sure as sunrise, his complaints would be heard before the day was over. Lucky for me, I was only a lieutenant, bottom of the officer rank ladder; he spared me in his declarations of the stupidity of the ideas.

I smiled inside when the men in the platoon complained about Broos' constant complaints. "Broos, why don't you shut the fuck up?" and "Can somebody shut Broos up?" were heard with regularity from the other men. He got on everyone's nerves, but he was a lightning rod within the platoon that deflected what could otherwise come my way. I really did like that bastard although he received my own sarcasm often enough.

16

Not long before dark, all eyes focused on a flight of five helicopters coming our way. They landed outside our perimeter, far enough away to keep the rotor-wash dust to a minimum. Some thirty men in full gear jumped from the choppers and walked in through our protective concertina wire. "Who the hell are they?" There was nothing normal about what I was seeing; strange shit was happening. Out of curiosity, I followed them as they walked to the company CP. They weren't my business, and I should have stayed at my bunker.

A platoon from Alpha company was sent in for a special mission, an ambush at the exact site we had four nights earlier; it made no sense to me. I knew every detail of the location. To make it easy for them, I briefed their lieutenant, and diagramed both the kill zone and the rear security layout for him.

"It'll be a piece of cake." I'd hardly gotten the words from my mouth when he asked the captain, "Do you have somebody who can guide us?"

My mind snapped to full alert, 'A guide!? Did he not hear anything I just told him? A guide? The fucking guy must be crazy.'

I kept my mouth shut. My eyes flicked to him, then to my captain, then back and forth. Immediately, without time for thought, the captain volunteered me to show them the way, to walk point for a platoon of strangers. I could almost see it coming and could have shot the stupid bastard right then and there and thought nothing of it.

'Does the man have any fucking brains at all? Any one of sixty fucking people in our company could find the fucking place blindfolded.' But he had to send me. 'Jesus Christ, Jesus H. Fucking Christ, that stupid son of a bitch.' I stood there in near shock, sure that he would realize what he had done, and change his order. I had been in country less than a month. I was a platoon leader, and he ordered me to walk point for a group of absolute strangers.

There was something not right about the whole operation for battalion to send another outfit into our area to pull an ambush in the exact spot we were in four days earlier. I thought, 'they must think we have some kind of fucking mental condition or something about going back down there. Hell, I had the kill zone then and there was Captain Dumbass sending me back with strangers, walking point. Shit, I wouldn't walk point for my own platoon; a point man walked point and I was not a point man; I was a goddamn platoon leader. That stupid fuck.'

There were two different types of units in the field: those that had their shit together, like we did, and those that stepped on their dicks, had casualties from carelessness. Who knew to which group this outfit belonged? Their platoon leader didn't show any fucking enthusiasm about the operation either. I could tell he didn't volunteer for the mission and was probably thinking like me, that something was screwed up.

I walked back to my platoon to let them know what was going on, what that dumb son of a bitch CO had done. With a surprised look on their faces, they shook their heads in empathy, knowing it was wrong, but no doubt thinking at the same time 'better him than me'; that's what any sane person would have thought. I grabbed my gear and stripped off all the shit except what I needed for the night – a half canteen of water, a couple of frag grenades, rifle and a shoulder bag full of magazines. 'Christ, that's why we had briefings; to mentally prepare ahead of time for missions, not to say "Hey, go grab your gear; you're moving out in five minutes for ambush."'

I took my time getting ready, not watching the speed of failing light. We should have been there by the time their last man cleared the wire. Fuck, it was already dusk, and we had a good fifteen or twenty minute walk ahead. Leaving late was just one more fucked up thing to go wrong.

I didn't give a rat's ass if it was my fault or not; from the corner of our large field, it was a straight shot to the ambush site, just like I told him. About fifteen hundred meters, a klick and a half, one mile down a wide, flat cart path would put us on the spot. Neither map nor compass was needed. There was only one landmark checkpoint; go straight to the T-intersection, stop, you're there. We headed out down the cart path beginning in one corner of the huge field where our NDP was located. We weren't supposed to be on it. If we got caught walking any path, road, or trail, I would be immediately relieved of duties and removed from the field. It would have been a form of military disgrace and punishment. Shit, maybe even their platoon leader would be too, for following me. Nobody was going to see us in the dark because we were damn sure the only ones out there. It was my decision to make. As far as I was concerned, it was the only way to get there. 'Fuck em, fuck all of them,' I thought.

I also realized that four nights earlier, nine gooks did exactly the same thing on the intersecting road and look what it got them - fucking dead. That was why only a fool would walk where we were walking. Once darkness started, it came on quick. I could remember every piece of terrain I had walked since we had been in that area and I knew what was in the front and on both sides, since I had been this way twice before. I wondered if the captain knew the consequences for walking it in the daytime. The left side had scrub undergrowth that gradually turned into chest-high grass near the abandoned hooches at the ambush site. The right side was marginally better but further down it was clear, bordered by three or four good-sized dry paddies.

The last of the light disappeared, and my mind shifted to the job at hand; we were moving smooth and slow through moonless dark. It was nearly silent, without a whisper or sound from a rifle sling or loose gear. All that could be heard was the soft shuffle of boots moving across the padded sandy dirt. The quietness made me feel better about whether they had their shit together or not. A snap came from our left side. I cocked my head and strained my ears the way an animal would at the unknown, hoping it was a nocturnal lizard or something similar moving. There were no follow up sounds like leaves rattling as if something was scurrying away. It was a loud snap and no more. My hearing was like a fucking bat. At night it missed nothing, making up for my imperfect night vision. I heard another snap. It was the same sound as a safety switch clicked off on a rifle.

It wasn't a single snap or even two. There was a series of them randomly spaced a few seconds apart, each one identical to the other as far as I could tell. I didn't like it and couldn't believe that many creatures could all make the exact noise, or break the same size twigs, but make no other sound. At the second snap, I froze mid-stride, the half-full canteen in my side pocket sounded akin to a breaking surf as the water sloshed inside. My knees began to shake, unstoppable; the water got louder. I had always thought 'knees shaking' was a joke, impossible to happen, but it could happen and there was nothing funny about it. Jesus Christ, the half-full canteen was loud. It was all I could hear. It was a goddamn fucking spooky situation. If ever I was scared in my life, it was then.

I restarted as quickly as I stopped, to quiet the canteen, telling myself 'It's just fucking lizards'. The snaps continued, and I veered right to the far edge of the cart path. I knew there was a small drop-off on that side, maybe twelve inches, if worse came to worst. I was counting on the men behind me to snake over behind me, each directly behind the other in the dark. We were spaced no more than two meters apart, instead of the five meters used during daylight. The consistency and number of the snaps gave me a bad feeling. I couldn't make myself believe it was nature, and I didn't want to believe that it was anything else.

My finger was on the trigger and thumb on the safety switch of the M-16 tucked under my arm. My heart was pounding. My thought was 'We may be in some real shit any second.' I was making as many mental calculations as I could. 'We would have maybe one full second, if lucky, to escape the worst, if the drop off on our right was deep enough.' I was aware how quickly it could come, the importance of less than a second.

I had counted the snaps, and the interval between them. There were six or seven. The one positive thought I had was any VC in there would know they were seriously outnumbered, and reserves not far away. They didn't have a winning hand either; not one could survive. My mind was running options at full throttle. Way too much was happening in my head. 'I could just open the fuck up and spray the left flank but the men behind me wouldn't be ready to follow suit. They would never be able to move quickly enough.' They had become my responsibility. We were single file, flanked, on flat ground; sure death for somebody. 'Jesus, don't let me die here so soon.'

I wished my own men were with me. I knew I could count on them. I was thinking how sorry I was to be there, how I should've stayed at my bunker. 'What am I even doing here?' It was impossible to not think about home. It kept popping through my head, images acting as involuntary muscles, forcing their way into consciousness. I was afraid I would never get the chance to say "I love you" one more time to my Sherry.

17

I felt unimaginable relief to get beyond the click sounds. I could only guess at the time the rear of the platoon was clear of the area.

Without moonlight, the only man I could see was a few feet behind when I arrived at the stopping point. We were just short of the intersection and the hooches, standing where the rear security would move in. The kill zone was further to our left front, another fifteen to twenty meters to the rear of the five deserted hooches that defined the kill zone.

'Jesus Christ, am I glad to be here. The grass and briars are probably still mashed down from where I was the other night.' I wasn't going to lie on that same patch again, and wanted off the front of that platoon.

I was eager to find their platoon leader and turn the mission back to him. My interest was limited to pointing toward the positions. My plan was to cease to have any function in the operation; from there, I was to be no more than extra baggage hanging out with them for the night.

I turned to my left to move back and locate their lieutenant, somewhere in the dark, when a single flash of a red-filtered flashlight caught the corner of my eye. There was no mistaking it. 'Shit! Goddamn it! VC'. It was angled away from me, but not enough that I didn't catch a glimpse. It was on the far side of exactly where the rear security would go.

I was tempted to open fire toward the light, but thought better. 'No, don't do that, the platoon is standing on open ground with zero cover. Fuck a body count.' There was no protection anywhere around the flat path for them in a firefight.

I moved back quickly, whispering, looking for the platoon leader, to make some plans. I was the only one who saw the light, thinking, 'Maybe we can spread out, lay down enough fire - call in the mortars ...' Hell, I didn't know a soul out there; it wasn't like I could say 'Dennis, take your men down there' or 'Rayborn, get ready to...' I didn't have a radio and didn't know if he was on our company frequency or not - if we could even call in our mortars.

He was already moving forward. Before I could say anything, a short burst of automatic weapon fire split the quiet. There was no muzzle flash, no tracer rounds. 'Where the fuck did that come from?' It was impossible to pinpoint the location in the split second, but it came from our left front, maybe from the intersecting cart path beyond the last hooch in the line. Maybe they were inside the end hooch, or they were down low in the grass of the field that stretched out on the river bottom land. I had patrolled the area twice, knew the landscape and was trying to think where they could be, if they had any cover, or were like us.

I suspected it was probably a meeting spot for messengers or guides. They weren't there for us. The burst wasn't toward us, more likely another signal to warn whoever was in the area. I was surprised they used the spot where we killed their local command group a few nights earlier. I don't know what we would have run into if we had been on time.

The platoon dropped to the ground with the burst. Thinking about the light, I still wasn't going to risk casualties by opening fire toward either the sound, or the red flash; there were too many unknowns. The idea of using the starlight scope to search for the flashlight position went through my head, but decided 'screw it'—it was not the time for a firefight. I was with strangers and in no mood to be heroic.

The battalion commander would have loved another body count, a little action, something he could proudly report up the chain, maybe hand out some medals to say 'Good job', add a little more padding on his command resume. 'Fuck him.'

The irony of the moment didn't escape me with the tables reversed, us walking down that path and the VC at our ambush site. I thought back to the earlier clicks and snaps, not so sure they were lizards after all. I never told my own men about the episode.

Their platoon leader radioed battalion, explained the situation, and a decision was made for us to move back into two dry rice paddies a short way behind us on the opposite side of the cart path. The plan suited the shit out of me. I guided them back to two large, dry paddies behind us and was damn glad it was over. Sometimes it was best to live and let live. Among strangers I preferred discretion.

I didn't mention the signal light to their lieutenant until the next morning, safely beyond any ideas of nocturnal heroism by anybody.

My adrenalin had been elevated since darkness fell. It seemed like forever. The operation was fucked-up from the plan's conception; battalion should've let our company take care of our own area when it came to ambushes.

Our stealthy retreat from the contact point went smooth. We backtracked and eased down the small drop-off into the sunken paddy.

I had barely stepped down when I walked into a low hanging limb. It stuck me straight in my left eye. "Jesus Christ," I mumbled. I wanted to scream and flail around like a

69

wounded Cyclops, but silence was the important thing. There was no end to the shit that day. I made no effort to crawl around and find their medic. Nobody was going to shine a flashlight in my eye out there that night, and I didn't need a medic to know that the cornea was scratched; it felt like a paper cut on the eyeball. The night was long and agonizing, spent with one hand covered an aching, throbbing eye.

I mainly thought of how much I despised that goddamn stupid son of a bitch company commander. The whole fucking night had been his fault as far as I was concerned. Both of us had been there for about three weeks. The last ounce of respect I had for that dumb bastard was gone; I was tired of his thoughtless whims that passed for decisions.

The sun striking my eye brought more misery than the dark. I was ready for medical attention when we got to the NDP, but it was not always so simple. The Army didn't believe in sickness or minor injury if you were in the field. About the only way to leave the field for medical attention was by Medevac, but I was in no mood for shit when I got back.

I dropped my gear and walked directly to the company CP, and told the captain I wanted to see a doctor. I was on a chopper before noon. The doc squeezed salve into it, and I was back on my way to the field in thirty minutes.

18

We didn't have any major stream crossings for several days. Our stay at the NDP had been almost two weeks. The time had come to consider a shower. The last had been at the water plant.

I had noticed the silhouette sticking up near the water cans: two vertical steel stakes with one wired horizontally across the top about seven feet above the ground. A five-gallon canvas bag with a shower head on the bottom hung from the top stake. It was rarely used by anyone; we didn't have much of a towel for bathing. All I had was the size of a hand towel and was used only as padding under gear straps, across the shoulders.

I clomped over in a pair of unlaced boots and pants to have a look at the contraption. Beneath the shower lay a wooden shipping pallet, to stay above of the mud while showering, and next to it were rows of metal five-gallon water cans brought out by a Chinook supply chopper. It wasn't hard to figure out how it operated: Remove the bag, hang it on a lower hook, fill it with a can of water, lift it back up to hang from the top stake. The large brass shower head unscrewed to turn on, or tightened to turn off. It looked like the head on an oversized garden sprinkler can. The green water cans sat under the full sun all day, a natural heater, creating a nice warm temperature that felt just right at dusk. 'Perfect' I thought. 'I should have done this before.' It was a contrast to how awful that same hot shit tasted coming out of a canteen during the day. We always had soap in our rucksack, mostly for shaving which we still had to do every day.

With a bar of soap in hand, the shower head was cracked open to get wet, then closed for soaping; it was better to conserve water rather than go through the process of refilling the bag. There was no reason to linger; the shower head was slightly above shoulder height, and it was an uncomfortable crouch to get under it. I hadn't noticed the occasional breeze gusting across our dirt field until I was standing on the pallet, in the open air, naked, wet and soapy. When the wind picked up, it dropped the water temperature to a few degrees below comfort. Before I could finish, I was in chill bumps, the wind gusted so hard the water no longer fell straight down. I was jumping around like an organ grinder's monkey, trying to stay under the blowing water. I was off the pallet, standing in the mud by the time I managed to get the soap rinsed and walked back to my bunker with muddy feet, carrying my boots. That was it concerning showers; it was easier to depend on stream crossings for baths, but I wanted to be decent for the next day. It was going to be special, I thought.

#

We had the usual evening briefing with the usual information: patrol checkpoint coordinates, point and drag platoon designations. It would be an air assault. My platoon would handle the insertion on the LZ and take the point for the day.

Then we had the big news of the briefing: A television news crew would be joining us the next morning. Fireworks swished and popped inside my head – how damn lucky could I get to have the point on that day – shit! It was CBS too; Walter

Cronkite! I looked as if I was studiously listening to the briefing, but the cogs were already turning in my head. I had watched Cronkite daily for months, mentally gathering and filing away visual glimpses of war news in his daily segments. I knew Sherry was doing the same, hurrying home from work at the hospital, hoping for one special day; her own glimpse – proof of my existence. I could imagine her ecstasy when November Platoon, Delta Company, 1st Battalion, 18th Infantry showed up on the Magnavox.

It was important to be clean and spiffy, ready for my date the next day with the CBS News camera crew. All I had to do was figure how get some camera time, but the point platoon leader should be able to do that without too much trouble. I was disappointed by the tone and brevity of the briefing. "Nobody in the company would speak, not one word, to them." The order came from above, but it was more like a veiled threat, not to be disobeyed. That put a dent in my plans, but still opportunity remained. Our special orders for silence indicated the press was not to be trusted, to be treated as a non-friendly necessity. Any communication with them would be handled through a Public Information Officer. 'Damn, what did PIO's know about the field?' I was too young, naive and ignorant to know the uneasy relationships between press, military, and government. I didn't know that Cronkite had declared the war unwinnable a few weeks before, following the Tet Offensive. I was in transit somewhere and hadn't seen the news in awhile. The only thing I was sure of was mud and dirt, sweat, mosquitoes, and a few Viet Cong. What he said didn't make any difference to us, anyway; it wasn't about to change our job.

#

The camera crew's chopper joined us after we were on the ground, and fell in near the rear of my platoon. I stayed near the rear too that day, and kept one eye on patrol business, the other craftily on them. We patrolled our normal rhythm and pace, they quietly followed without interference. Out of curiosity, I kept watch on the camera operator. He was a wiry Vietnamese about the same stature as Charlie Mi, and it was a rough day for travel through fucking mud and water. I admired his agile, surefooted balance and endurance hauling the bulky camera on his shoulder; he never faltered. I hoped he was well paid.

It was a short patrol distance on the map, but a water-crossing about thirty feet across, along with the other shit conditions, made for a long day. We picked a shady spot to cross where the slope of the banks allowed us to get in and out with the least effort. One by one the men slipped down the bank, keeping hold of the span of rope, submerging to their necks, pulling themselves across hand over hand. It was a slow go. My time got close. I dumped everything I wanted to keep dry from my pockets: matches, C-ration toilet paper, Marlboros, map – all things precious. Like every man would do before crossing, items were carefully wedged and tucked under the heavy elastic band that held the camouflage cover on my helmet. As we milled around waiting, I saw the camera man set up for his shots of the water-crossings and knew it was my only opportunity. I cared less about appearing on the news other than to somehow get a message home anyway I could. Since we weren't allowed to speak, just my face would say 'Here I am and here's what I'm doing today. I'm okay'.

I was looking at what the camera operator could see moving through the watery shade, nothing more than the backs of helmets and two arms sticking out of the water. With my M-16 slung over my shoulder, I slid down the slick bank that had become a mud slide. Part way across, I turned sideways enough to offer a profile to the camera position, hoping to be identifiable if it showed up on the news. It was a long shot, but it was all I had.

By mid-afternoon, we had moved out to a dry area for the crew to catch their chopper. Once again, they set up the camera for a sign off. They stood in front of a few dried-out, long deserted hooches. In the process, someone in their group made a not too vague suggestion that we might set fire to what was left of the tinder-box constructions. They would have gone 'poof' – like a match stick, surely offering a spectacular background for them, while we would look like mindless vandals. The men looked around at each other, eyebrows raised or a slight smile, saying nothing. The answer was 'no'. We would not set fire to them, deserted or not. The very idea was stupid. Why the hell would we start a useless fire while standing in the hot sun? I thought, 'Those fucking people are nuts.' It was one of those little flash moments in life. My skepticism of the press began. I saw another facet of their job; enhanced news – entertainment value – that may or may not represent truths. It was understandable for them to want exciting footage, but it wasn't going to happen at our expense. They got film of the real war that day, the 99.9% of it, the boredom, sweat, heat, mud, water, nothingness. It probably wasn't good for ratings.

I stood less than ten feet from the reporter, who I didn't recognize. He signed off with 'from outside a VC village' or some kind of horse shit like that. It was all I could do to not jump between him and the camera screaming, "It was nothing but some old abandoned hooches," as if he didn't know. It may have been deserted because of the VC, even likely, but that day it was nothing. I was biting my tongue, remembering our orders for silence, unsure of what would happen to me if they saw me speaking on film. I would have told him, "If there was VC around, we would find them" and "we killed nine of them in a perfect fucking ambush six days ago, and I had been scared witless two nights before while walking point in the black". I would have told him the truth about all of it, the real truth; not some metaphorical bullshit about 'a VC village'. Unfortunately, I was ordered not to talk

#

I didn't have to see the news story on TV to know that when Walter Cronkite signed off with his daily 'and that's the way it is', it was a lie that day. He didn't know I knew, but I did. I was standing there. I walked away, my allusion of the news altered. I continued to watch the CBS Nightly News with Cronkite after my return home to see what was happening in the war. At the same time, I never believed everything I saw or heard a full one hundred percent.

Back in the NDP that evening, I could hardly wait to grab my pen and writing pad; it was my number one priority. Full of hope, I fired off my daily letter filled with word to watch for me, or our unit, on the TV. Our mail was fast, even back then, but the film was quicker than my letter. Sherry was running a little late getting to the apartment that day; the TV was always turned on the news the instant she walked in. The war film segment had already begun, and the introduction information was missed, but she thought the head sticking out of the water looked like me. At the end, they mentioned the company commander's name, Captain Shaw. I had mentioned his name in an earlier letter, but she thought it was 'Snow', so still she wasn't totally sure. Despite having decent penmanship my whole life, when using my knees, sandbags or a steel helmet as a writing desk, usually trying to write in half dark, it turned it into barely decipherable scribble. In an effort to see it again, to know if her eyes were correct or deceived, she called the local CBS affiliate station in Nashville. "Sorry ma'am, we only provide a feed and don't have copy." She received my letter the next day or two confirming everything she saw. We couldn't tie all the information together until we met on R&R several months later, and it no longer mattered a hell of a lot by then. The film clip was never seen again. If you ever see an old CBS news story from March 24, 1968, from Vietnam, watch for the head in profile. "…And that's the way it was."

19

The questions are fiction. The answers are not.

Of course they didn't, but would it have been too much for the press to come home with us? They could've hung out a couple of days instead of flying out and spending each day with a different unit. This is a 'what if they'd done that' interview.

I'd have said, "Hey man, come on in, have a seat. What do you want to know?"

Q. Okay, how long have you been here?
A. Just about one month. To be exact, I would have to count the Xs on my calendar with the picture of Jesus on the back.

Q. Jesus huh? Do you think about Jesus much out here in the field?
A. When I need to, I guess, you know - after the pucker factor kicks in on your ass.

Q. What about other times for religion?

A. We had a chaplain come out and give services one day. I don't know if it was a Sunday or not. I don't keep up with days of the week like that; just Xs. It could have been on a Wednesday.

It seemed funny, everybody standing out in the open, in the middle of the NDP, singing and praying. It was good insurance, you know, and it looked good for the men to see me there. I kept thinking, 'Don't sing too loud. One good fucking mortar round could kill most of the company standing there.' I knew where the nearest bunker was. I was anxious for it to be over; I was thankful for a brief service. My radio operator probably enjoyed it.

Q. Why him?

A. Keller? His father is a Texas preacher – Baptist, I think – and I suspect Keller is a lot like him. He doesn't say much to me. We don't exactly speak the same language. I'll bet he secretly prays for me every day, or he may not. Could be the other way around, that he doesn't give a shit – either way, he does a good job.

Q. What about your other men?

A. What? I know their home states, and if they are married or not, but that's about it. If possible, I'll try to keep married men, especially with kids, off the edges on patrols.

Q. Ages? Whether they are draftees or volunteers, things like that?

A. None of that stuff matters a rat's ass to me. I don't know theirs, they don't know mine. As for the other, I figured most of them are drafted like me, but that doesn't matter either; you do your fucking job and hope to get back home. That's the name of the game, as far as I can tell.

I do like to know when somebody is getting close to going home, but that's never a problem – all you hear for weeks is the fucker saying 'short-timer' and how many Xs are on his calendar, or how many days are left in-country. But I want to know if a good experienced man is leaving soon, who's going to step in to replace him; those guys are invaluable and I hate to see them go, but they've done their time.

I wish they would send us a class clown, somebody to put in charge of morale, make guys laugh. We don't have a good morale man, but we have one that helps in that department – Tex. He's from Mississippi, and don't think he ever lived in Texas. I have no idea why the hell they call him Tex, but he's funny and cheerful. I have a couple of dipshits, though, who are anti-morale.

Q. How does that happen?

A. They are the ones who are as much nuisance as help, somebody like Hiedricks. He's from Brooklyn or the Bronx, somewhere up there. The snaggle-toothed bastard's mouth runs non-stop when we're in the NDP, plus he has a harmonica that he can't play. He just makes noise and gets threats from the men 'to shut the fuck up' if he won't be quiet. And, of course, we have Broos, our resident complainer who gets on most nerves, but not mine. Maybe we're too much alike. Everybody grumbles at one time or another, but we're all in it together. I consider most complaining good; it means they are actually happy in a way because they can let off steam verbally, and they'll do a good job. I complain too when I think things are worse than need be.

Q. Is Vietnam what you expected?

A. Visually it is. I had seen enough pictures, heard the stories, but training only gets you so far. On my level, war is war. I think it doesn't matter which war it is, settings and environments change. Attila the Hun's soldiers probably had the same general thoughts as us. At least I'm not in the Korean

War. I would've hated that fucking cold; I don't know how those guys stood it. I have an uncle who was a grunt in Korea - got three fingers shot off.

I am kind of surprised by some of the dumb-ass shit we do, operation-wise, but hey, I just follow orders, not make them. I guess it's been that way in every war though.

Q. What do you mean? Dumb operations?

A. It's just that if we see or find something promising, some lead to track down VC, it won't matter if it's time to move on; it's like we are always on a fucking schedule, fucking war on a fucking schedule. I don't care if we get in an hour late, if we have a good reason to stay out. I would have camped out by the village the day that Charlie Mi questioned an old man about cooking so much food. I would have had an ambush around there to find out what was going on. I didn't expect the 'no time to do our job' mentality, gotta move on. It is stupid. We are here to fight, so why don't we track them down instead of accidentally running into them?

Q. Is it the commanders' faults?

A. I don't know who controls what. All I know is what goes on out here, in our company. Plain common sense about things would be nice.

Q. Is that lacking? Common sense?

A. I haven't been here that long, but it seems in short supply at the top. I haven't seen any yet.

Q. By officers or who?

A. In the platoon, the ones with common sense are listened to by most, myself included. The combination of experience and common sense can keep people alive. The other platoons? I don't know; I seldom talk to the other platoon leaders. We don't socialize out here. The second platoon leader seems okay, but the little rat-faced bastard that runs the first platoon is a sorry ass; he hangs his water on his radio man's back pack, while humping around on patrol. He then laughs about not having to carry the weight. Fuck him.

Q. What about the company commander?

A. He got here a few days after me. I think he's a useless fucker; I don't see or talk to him except at daily briefings. I guess he figured out by now I don't like him. He's in the wrong place out here as a company commander, but why should he care? There are always thirty men between him and shit. He's like a capricious brat that makes arbitrary decisions.

I hate to say it, but he gives ROTC a bad name. He's the stereotype everybody thinks of about ROTC officers. It made no difference to me when he got here, but Jesus, nobody out here likes the son of a bitch. I thought it was just me for awhile, but it's the whole fucking company.

Q. How do you know?

A. Radios. We were out on patrol one day, hot and bored, when Keller, my Kilo, that's what we call radio operators, says 'Listen to this'. He is always a few meters away – we don't walk close together – so I ease over and he cranks the volume up a little. In a few seconds, there's a voice: 'Shaw sucks'. A minute later there's another, then another and it sounded like bullfrogs sitting around a pond in the summertime, all croaking the same.

I smiled, but was thinking, 'This shit is not good for him'. They monitored all company radios at battalion headquarters and I was thinking that kind of sentiment might get him transferred out to another unit, or job. There are about fifteen radios in the three platoons, so they can't be tracked down. It got to be a daily ritual for awhile and he had to have gotten the message. It made me feel better just knowing I wasn't the only one. I didn't encourage it in my platoon, but didn't say 'don't do it' either.

Q. Did you volunteer for Vietnam?

A. I actually out-smarted myself from day one. There was physically nothing wrong with me when I was drafted, and had what they called a 'picket fence profile' because each box across the page had a number one. I figured I was coming here anyway. That was my first miscalculation. If I'd kept my mouth shut, I'd had orders for MP (Military Police) School, but after I said yes, I was sent to Infantry. At the time it sounded better to make five hundred dollars a month than one-fifty. I was married, so I volunteered for OCS and here I am. Hell, I never heard of OCS before I was drafted; didn't even know I took a test for it.

Q. How long have you been married?

A. About a year and a half; I got my draft notice nine days before our wedding, and the fifth morning after I climbed on the Greyhound. Everything was ready for the wedding, too late to change anything. There was a good size group of us draftees that morning; some of the guys I'd gone to school with.

Q. You have eleven months left. Any thoughts?

A. I think I'm ready to go home now. I've seen all the war I need already, or I would hang around to be a photographer; that's what I'd rather be. I look at our tall two-niner-two antenna every evening I'm here, at the silhouette and think that is symbolic of war. It looks desolate. I don't know why, it's just our antenna that reaches battalion or beyond, maybe twenty feet tall, with guy wires, but the black silhouette just reaches up, nothing around it.

I'll meet my wife in Hawaii on R&R for our second anniversary in five months, and hope to be home six months after that. That's about as large a chunk of time as I can think of right now. I don't have enough Xs on my calendar to officially start counting yet – too much white space left. When it gets dark, I think 'another day gone'. That's about it.

20

The words echoed around the NDP. "Pack up, we're leaving." Air mattresses were deflated and rolled, poncho roofs disassembled, and rucksacks filled. The men moved with a bounce in their steps when they heard the destination was DiAn, a huge rear base and home for Delta Company. We were going to spend the night; there was almost a cheer.

It had been nearly six months for some since their last trip into the home base where the barracks were located. It was a treat for them. I had only been out for a month and it made little difference about going into DiAn, but I was ready to leave for new places.

Dropping their gear in the barracks, men with soap and shampoo hit the showers and came out scrubbed with hair combed and parted, and wearing clean fatigues. They were as happy as a bunch of school girls going to a party. Some were hardly recognizable. Then they scattered like wind-blown dandelion seeds to the PX for personal resupply, barber shop, and all around taking care of needs.

Sleeping on a bed with a mattress, and outdoor, warm, running-water showers were first class treats. A sunset grill-out with steaks and chicken, and two jeep trailers filled with iced beer and soft drinks was a homecoming celebration. It was a time to unwind, smile, laugh, sit on chairs at a table covered up with hot food and cold beers. It was a night to write letters home, sitting under a light bulb, using paper and envelopes not covered in dust and dirt.

#

The grind returned the next morning; we repacked and waited at the chopper pad – destination Lai Khe, home to division headquarters. We would have our assignment briefing after arrival.

Chinooks were our transportation. I hadn't ridden on one. Once was enough, equivalent to riding in a sky truck on a bumpy road. To say it was better than walking was about all I could about them. They always reminded me of big green, flying bananas. They had huge rotors on each end, and a tail ramp that dropped down for entry and exit.

Walking up the ramp into the cavernous cargo area, the platoon split, each half facing one another, sitting on the floor, backs against the sides of the fuselage. We loaded one platoon per chopper with room to spare. The cumbersome layers of equipment each man carried stayed on his back; it was uncomfortable as hell. The joyous night before had been forgotten.

The twin rotors powered up. It shook, vibrating through the floor into every bone of my body from that point until we landed. Overwhelming noise stopped any and all chance for conversation. The platoon looked like a load of mutes with expressionless faces. It must have been a thirty to forty minute flight. There was no need to check my watch; we'd get there when we got there.

It wasn't our last Chinook ride, and I learned a lesson for future reference. On all other flights I sat at the bottom of the loading ramp, facing forward. I could lean back against the closed, sloping cargo ramp with my gear and rucksack, pull my knees up toward my chest, getting all my limbs and body parts wedged, triangulated, and counterbalanced into a lump. Using my fingers as earplugs, I could cat nap for a few minutes.

#

"This is the kind of place I'll like," I said, standing on the Lai Khe chopper pad. Of course I already had a full description by the platoon old-timers who had been that way a time or two before. Usually it was Sergeant Dennis who couldn't wait to tell me everything about new places; he was one part travel agent and tour guide. Although foretold, I couldn't imagine what it would be like standing in the middle of rubber trees. Shade was heaven, pure and simple.

The base was partially located in an old rubber plantation. Equally spaced trees in straight rows, from all perspectives provided a cooling, dappled shade and gloriously dry ground. The simple pleasure of standing beneath the high canopies, enjoying light breezes while talking was such a relief from the low, sun-battered makeshift poncho roofs of the past two weeks. It was too bad there were no plans to leave us in that, or any other level of comfort.

The men were on free-time most of the day. The majority headed to the village outside the wire to look around, visit whorehouses or get blow jobs, taking full advantage of local enterprise, whatever it was. I didn't make it, but they made it sound like a midway at a state fair.

I was briefed that afternoon for that night, as well as the location for our next NDP. Neither was promising.

They stuck us on berm guard that night, securing a sector of the base perimeter. I couldn't believe the size of the place until we loaded on trucks and rode for ten minutes. Three men jumped off at two-hundred meter intervals. That was the spacing between bunkers. They were huge, the size of small conex shipping containers with thick sod roofs, easily large enough for twice the number of men. Fields of fire were cleared about a hundred meters to the front, where a chain-link and concertina wire fence edged the thick bush beyond.

It all went fine until about ten o'clock. Three or four rounds popped off from one of the bunkers down the road to my right. I cringed. "There goes some dipshit." It was one of my men, and whether they were spooked or firing just for the fun, it was stupid.

Within seconds the captain was on the radio. "Who's doing the firing down there?" I knew what was coming. Nobody cared but him.

I responded. "Delta 6; November 6 – Roger. I think that was in the second platoon's area." That excuse didn't work. The second platoon leader came on the radio. His call sign was Mike 6.

"Uh, Delta 6; this is Mike 6. That's a negative. The shots did not come from my area. Out."

Delta 6 called back. "November 6, this is Delta 6." I knew what he was going to say before he got the words out of his mouth. "Go down your positions and find out what's going on."

"Can you believe this dumb ass?" I asked in the usual rhetorical thinking out loud, although my RTO and medic were in there too.

"Delta 6, November 6. Roger that." 'Roger' meant that I understood his message. I looked at my watch for a time-check and explained my plan. "If that dumb son-of-a bitch thinks I'm going to walk around out there this time of night, he's out of his fucking mind. Some idiot in the next bunker would probably shoot my ass at the first noise he heard."

If Shaw thought I would walk two hundred meters to the next bunker, he should've thought to send up some artillery flares too, because that was the only way it would happen. The man was brainless. I sat outside, up on top of the bunker enjoying what little air stirred, smoked a Marlboro or two for about twenty minutes, then got back on the radio.

"Delta 6; November 6 – Over."

"November 6, this is Delta 6."

"Roger, I went down and checked. A man thought he heard something out by the wire, popped off a few rounds. Over."

"Roger, Delta 6 out."

…And so it went, with horse-shit like that.

21

It was close to noon when we moved to the chopper pad to head out of Lai Khe. We had one final briefing that morning about the insertion for the new NDP.

"The LZ area will be prepped with artillery fire for several hours before we arrive." It was a new experience for me and an ominous feeling.

It sounded like a hell of a lot of overkill, enough to pique my interest. How bad could the place be? I didn't make the connection instantly, but this was going to be a battalion-size NDP instead of our usual company-size. That meant about four hundred or more men, plus battalion headquarters. All that artillery wasn't particularly for us. Naturally, battalion headquarters wanted to feel safe.

In fact, when we arrived at our LZ later, I never saw evidence of one fucking artillery round landing anywhere around our location. There were no trees showing hits that I could see as we went in on the choppers, nor a crater mark on the ground. I'd have bet battalion had a different LZ, well prepped.

The briefing had some new twists. At the LZ, thirty or forty meters to our right, will be chainsaws, axes, picks, and cans of gas, left there by advance Reconnaissance Patrols.

The area looked bad enough on my map, nothing but grids of green: no water, no villages, towns or roads, other than the one we would be on. The singular road was north-south Highway 13, our infamous Thunder Road. There was nothing else on the map to indicate where we might be; it was damn sure out the hell from nowhere best I could tell.

By the time all the information from the briefing was in my head, I had to wonder who came up with the idea for the whole operation. It sounded like something the Battalion Commander would plan as another exercise in military resume enhancement for himself. He was more like a politician anyway. He didn't belong in the field and it looked disingenuous from what I had seen of him. The field took a different mind-set than he was used to in his normal, safe headquarters locations. His place was in his LOH, observing from the air where everything looked nice and neat. My impression was that he could never be either feral or primal; those were requirements in the field.

We were fully briefed, ready to load up and go. Second platoon would take the point from the LZ. We would be in the rear, pick up and carry the extra equipment. That was reasonable. They would mash enough underbrush down to make a path for us. Some of the men would be hauling close to a hundred pounds. I thought 'how can that get fucked up?' Ask the CO.

22

The LZ was a narrow, red clay road cut through a dense wooded landscape. It was the only place to land. From the air, the tree canopy made the ground invisible. Escorted in by gunships on the flanks, the landing was uneventful. We were on Highway 13, one of the two major routes north from Saigon.

The men found our stash of tools well-hidden in some bushes, exactly where they were supposed to be. A distribution of the forty-five pound cans of gas, a heavy chainsaw, and heavy duty picks and axes were given to whoever had a free hand and was strong enough to carry them. We had gotten in front of the second platoon on the LZ, and were ready to step to one side and let them file by to lead us in.

Despite the company briefing, with the same information passed on down to every man in my platoon, and plans made, a new decision was made. The CO changed the order of point. We would now have point. Fine, my response was, "we'll set the tools down and second platoon can carry them."

"Negative, you carry the equipment too," the capricious bastard said.

I was seething inside, thinking 'What if we have contact?' We were screwed. With full gear and ruck sacks, the men had to sling their weapons over their shoulders, using both hands to carry extra shit. What a fucking brainless idiot.

I wasn't really worried about contact; we were moving a short distance, but he should have thought about our security. The dumb fucker never thought about anything. We traveled parallel to the road which was only a few meters on our left flank, but it was against operational procedures to walk it.

The map showed the distance to the NDP, but not the terrain. It turned out to be six hundred meters of thick, tangled undergrowth and vines that tripped and caught on everything. The men carrying extra weight constantly swapped off every few feet; we were barely moving forward.

I could see Palmer, our point man, from my position; he was loaded as light as possible, still about fifty pounds, fighting for every step. Suddenly he stopped and started slinging everything off: weapon, rucksack, gear then clothes. I moved closer to see what was wrong. His normal blond hair was solid red, as was the rest of his head, down to the top of his shoulders. He had bumped a small tree that had a red ant nest attached, and they dropped straight down on him by the hundreds, if not thousands.

The men directly behind dropped their own equipment to help Palmer strip, grabbing clothes and gear, slapping and shaking everything out, moving it to a safe spot.

Every man in the field hated those fucking ants. The color of boiled lobster, they clamped their pincers shut on skin and their bodies stood straight out from its head, rear legs and tail-end in the air. They were fierce little creatures.

I had never seen them above the ground. The nest was made from the biggest leaves from nearby trees, overlapped and sealed along the edges, the general shape of a large football. Bright green, it was perfectly camouflaged in the foliage, attached to a low limb on the sapling. The nest remained covered by guards, standing erect on their hind legs, pincers open toward us, defiant of our presence.

It took a hell of a lot longer than expected to reach our company's area of responsibility in the NDP. Two men had physically dropped from exhaustion by the time we reached the edge of the clearing. When I entered the opening, if I wasn't already in a war zone, I would have described our new site as looking like a war zone.

It was a hellish circle, hundreds of meters in diameter. Rome plows had been at work. The Rome plow was a large bulldozer with a special blade attached to the front, used to push down trees as a means to clear forests. The trees had been uprooted, lying across the entire area like so many oversized toothpicks dropped and left to lie.

We had to travel to the far side of the opening to reach our area. Travel was only marginally easier as we wove our way around large root balls or crawled over fallen trees.

I hated the shit-hole of a place from the time we walked in until we packed up and left. There were only two advantages, as far as I could tell. It was dry and mosquito free. I doubted mosquitoes could find enough out there to survive on, but I carried my repellent anyway.

23

Travel was six hundred meters in forty-five minutes, less than a mile per hour. We reached the opening where the battalion would be moving: our destination was on the far side. The platoons had no shortage of medics so a couple of them were left behind to revive the exhausted men.

It was impossible to walk towards our sector without stepping and crawling over, or around fallen trees and roots. 'The place is a goddamned disaster.' Questions about why we needed chainsaws and axes were answered by the time we traversed the open span. We dropped our gear on the arc of the imaginary circle that our company would occupy.

In amazement, I looked at our new home. It was going to be a challenge to find usable spots to dig in bunkers and maintain overlapping fields of fire.

Our building start was interrupted. As soon as we stripped ourselves of gear, I got orders from the captain to make a cloverleaf reconnaissance patrol, five hundred meters in front of our new area. I left a handful of men back to get bunker positions laid out and organize a work plan.

Before heading out, I told the ones left behind, "You listen for us and don't shoot our asses when we come back in." You couldn't leave such simple things unsaid. In a new place, tired men with weapons kept close and no shortage of ammunition, it was a worthwhile reminder. Bad things were known to happen in situations like that; we were only a handful of meters to the wood line and beyond that, visibility was almost nil. They were more likely to hear something before seeing it.

The remainder of the platoon left every piece of non-essential equipment behind, and light-loaded with weapons with a bag full of ammo, for our quick recon. After we had been on the move for awhile, with one eye on my watch, I asked our distance man, "How far are we?"

"About three hundred meters," he said. One man in the platoon always stepped off our distance on patrols; without physical landmarks to identify, it was the only way to know our position on the map coordinates. It seemed like we had traveled further in the slow going of the thick underbrush. Not as bad as our walk-in from the LZ, but it was too thick for effective tactical operations; I wasn't worried about VC coming in from that direction. It was good to know what the area looked like.

"Okay, fuck it, we're far enough. This is all the same. Time to split." Half the platoon went left, half to the right. "Circle out no more than a hundred meters and loop back in – and whatever you do, goddamn it, don't shoot at any fucking noise. If you don't see it, don't shoot." It may seem like a lot of unnecessary foul language. Maybe it was, but it was used to underline what was said. I didn't want anybody getting shot by some dumb fucker. It also let them know I was not in a screw-around mood. I figured a couple of hundred meters between us would keep anybody from shooting each other because of hearing noises. Soldiers had been known to get 'mis-oriented', an infantry euphemism for lost. In the worst situations, it was a good way to get killed.

We were back to our perimeter within forty-five minutes. The other two platoons were working full speed. I asked the men who stayed back how the other platoons got so far along. "They never left, been there working the whole time." The low-life, sorry son-of-a-bitch Shaw sent only us out, after he had reversed his earlier briefing for point into the site. "The bastard fucked us twice in one day" was the platoon consensus, and it was never forgotten. It was the last straw in his inept ability to lead. I never spoke to him again outside necessity in briefings and on the radio. He was a black cloud that hung over the company, no longer deserving respect; nobody gave a shit about his rank.

It was two hours from dark, not a hole dug yet. Sergeant Rayborn was carving out bunker positions with the chainsaw, then moving to clear fields of fire to the tree line, less than fifty meters out. Blocks of C-4 explosive loosened up the tougher problems of root balls still partially submerged. Everybody else manned axes and picks, ripping strands of tree roots out of the ground, and shovels, digging holes and filling the sandbags brought with us. Each man had ten bags rolled and tied to his rucksack; more came in on supply choppers. A slit-trench latrine still needed to be dug, and our perimeter wire had to in place before nightfall. Rolls of coiled concertina wire were waiting for us to pick up at the chopper pad. At twilight, men stopped digging to stretch and stake in place the concertina wire to form our outer security. Sounds of shovels continued into the blackness, working quietly. I quit at 0200, some kept pace until 0500. We had a four-hour patrol, moving out at eight.

With the patrol back, the afternoon was dedicated to finishing work. Tiredness set in, and enthusiasm for defeating our personal wasteland of wood debris faltered. Grunts were always practical thinkers when it came to lightening workloads, and one of the men came up with the idea of burning the logs to clear our area. That sounded better than chainsaws and axes. Why not? We already had gas for the chainsaw. Why not use it to start things burning? Unfortunately it was like trying to burn out stumps; the fucking logs only smoldered without flame. It was a windless day. Smoke hung like a fog, hardly reaching head height. Work continued, but we were unable to breathe without gas masks, adding more emphasis to the heat. When we left two weeks later, the charred logs lay where they were when we walked in.

#

Highway 13 bisected the encampment. I walked to the center of it one day, looked one direction, turned and looked in the opposite direction. It was straight as far as I could see each way, smooth and unused. It was a surreal, perfectly engineered ghost road without a tire mark on it; convoys didn't run the highway in that area. It was the upper part of the Iron Triangle; the VC controlled the area as much as anyone.

24

Our operational environment was the exact opposite of the place we recently left. We swapped the mud and water for masses of entanglements that were going to be a pain in the ass every day. The differences were obvious, and I never thought how it might affect some of the men. It made no difference to me, I was happy to be out of the sun and mud.

Our entire routine of operating was changed. My own work load became lighter. I had nights off and more days off, too. Battalion headquarters decided to use squad-size ambushes instead of the platoon. The battalion operations officer was a Major. I didn't know him, but it was not evident that he had ever served in a company-level command position, either as company commander or platoon leader. The whole platoon would get the day off because of the smaller ambushes, but was a mistake to use under-strength squads for ambushes. We were down to seven or eight men per squad, and in that number were new, inexperienced men.

The switch from flat open areas, where the men were used to long, clear visual fields, to the claustrophobic feel of the closed-in bush had its effect on small squads at night. An eight man squad meant a maximum of four positions for an ambush to cover three-hundred and sixty degrees. That was not good for those used to being part of a full platoon ambush formation.

One of the first ambushes assigned was to a mostly green squad, including a new squad leader. They were about five hundred meters out, a close-in ambush by any measure. It had been dark a few minutes on one of those moonless, black nights that served to amplify conditions and situations. The squad reported hearing noises. In seconds, claymores exploded toward the ghosts inhabiting their imagination. Following procedures, they were called back to the NDP.

Word passed from bunker to bunker. "Hold your fire; men coming in."

I stood at the wire, waiting, knowing what had happened. They got spooked. Following a head count and equipment check as they filed through the wire, I asked, "Where's the starlight scope?"

The answers went like this: "I thought he had it." "No, I don't have it. I put it back next to you" – back and forth horseshit, nobody willing to say 'We just wanted to get the fuck out of there'. They left it at the ambush site.

"Fuck! Goddamn it! You mean it's still out there?" The scope was our primary advantage for night operations, allowing us to see in the dark, and damn sure something we couldn't allow to fall in the hands of the VC... not to mention the cost of $3500.00. I felt like sending them back out right then to find it.

I stayed off the radio and walked to company headquarters to report the situation. I didn't want the other platoons and battalion listening to such a major fuck-up. Everybody around already had enough radio entertainment for one night. The whole night was turning into bad mojo. I'd rather gone out on platoon-size ambushes than have the shit that was happening. It had gone well beyond the ten percent factor.

There was only one solution. Our mortar platoon pumped out a half dozen 'white phosphorous', known as Willy Peter, rounds on top of their ambush site to destroy the scope, or at least burn it enough make it inoperable. I wasn't sure if we could get a new one.

I was still hot, if not worse, when I got back to our platoon sector, unfinished with the squad leader. "Goddamn it, it was in your hand went you left. It was supposed to be in your hand coming back. Now we're going to be without a fucking scope. The mortar platoon is getting ready to cover the area with WP rounds, there won't be shit left when that goddamn Willy Peter hits it. At first light, you will take your squad back out there and retrieve whatever is left of it."

'What a fucking bunch' I thought. 'Between the dumb-ass idea of sending a squad out in this thick shit to start with, and... Jesus Christ, I sat down with them and went over the whole fucking thing in every little detail before they went out that night, to make sure they were okay. A goddamn piece of cake and they fuck it up.' Even when their eyes looked calm, saying they understood everything, I knew their stomachs were rolling. I could feel it.

A half-hour before daylight, the sky and trees were coming into shades of blackish gray, I stood at the wire again as they filed back out through the wire. Moving fast, it wasn't long before their shapes appeared through lighter shades of gray, scope in hand. It didn't have a mark on it. It made me wonder where the fucking mortar rounds landed, or if the squad was even in the right spot, but grateful to have the starlight back in one piece; it was best to speak no more about it. I told the mortar platoon leader about the results. We both shrugged our shoulders. What the fuck.

As much as I'd hoped the platoon learned something, it wasn't the only screw-up. A few nights later, our platoon LP (Listening Post), two or three men sitting not more than fifty meters outside the wire, radioed they were seeing flashlights moving. "Where are they?" I asked.

"They're all around us." I spent fifteen or twenty minutes on the radio to get them calmed down and convince them it was fireflies, not VC roaming around the bush with flashlights. "I can see them too" I told them, although I couldn't. The fact that they were moving vertically too, rather than a horizontal line finally brought them rational thoughts.

#

Our patrols were the normal two-platoon size. Some covered easily passable areas, while some were a day of vine undergrowth similar to our arrival. I was relieved to have the luck of being the rear platoon on the days of tough going, feeling sorry for the poor bastards up front, knowing what they were up against. Enemy contact, or any sign of them in the area was non-existent, but they were there and they knew we were there.

One night, directly across the perimeter, one of the companies got hit with incoming mortar rounds. Instinctively, we dove into our nearest bunkers, too. Some had two men, some four or five packed in; they were only large enough for three men. I barely escaped injury when Private Brickles gave me a shove, head first into a bunker, determined to save my life from mortars hitting three or four hundred meters away. "Goddamnit Brickles, were you trying to kill me! I couldn't even move with people piled on top of me."

"I was just trying to help."

"Well, don't try to help me again. I can get in a fucking bunker on my own - feet first."

#

Nearing the last hour or two of our patrol one afternoon, we were intercepted by a Long Range Reconnaissance Patrol (LRRP). They were known as Lurps. Three- or four-man teams, they spent extended periods in boonies collecting intelligence on the enemy. Their mission was not to engage. That day they were looking for help to fill their empty canteens. They stood to one side of our patrol filing by, holding canteens out with tops off. Every man who passed, and had water, poured some into their canteens; they were appreciative.

A couple of months later, word came around there was an opening in the Lurps, and Sergeant Rayborn was itching to sign up. He thought one way then the other about signing up. It was a semi-glory job, a way to avoid the daily grind of patrols and ambushes; they operated with more freedom. He finally asked my opinion. He wasn't my favorite squad leader, but he was experienced. He had his good points and I was terribly low on manpower, as usual. I neither encouraged nor discouraged him, but did remind him of a couple of things. We had hot chow every chance it could be gotten to us, and about those guys standing out in the bush, asking for water. He decided he liked the platoon after all. Later, the lucky fucker escaped death by sitting in the right spot in the back of a three-quarter ton truck that hit a mine.

#

We had an unusual day when my platoon had point and patrolled through areas yet to be invaded by all things growing to prevent our movement. The whole area was shaded and free of undergrowth, with clear vision more than ten feet in any direction.

Our point man walked upon two wires running perpendicular to our direction of travel. Small, different colors, they obviously were laid intentionally. I was thinking, 'They could only have one of two uses, either land-lines for communications, or remote firing detonator wires for the big 120mm rockets.' I couldn't understand the need for such long wires to rockets in an area that desolate, but if they were communication, it could mean there were encampments or transit bivouac areas around. Regardless, it was an area clear enough that VC or NVA (North Vietnamese Army) troops could operate with little problem; there were no US military bases around and the solid canopy from the trees gave cover.

Palmer held up. I stopped the patrol, looked around and radioed back to the CO what we had found. Travel was easy that day, and we had time to investigate. I wanted to check the area. I didn't like the idea of splitting the platoon, but was ready to send a squad each direction, to follow the wires for five minutes to see where they might lead. The rest of the platoon would stay in place, to move quickly if either patrol ran into trouble. My mental radar was already in full alert, apprehensive, thinking we might track down a nice weapons cache, base camp, equipment, something... anything. It was the closest we had been to contact. Somebody had run those wires and that meant there was an end to them somewhere.

Nope, it wasn't to be the case. The bastard commander, vacuous of normal military concern, was well content to keep going: finish the patrol. I believed my question had been answered about why some of the other companies seemed to have a magnet for significant action. Maybe they kept their eyes open, followed their noses sometime. I'd rather have gone out on platoon size patrols and let the useless bastard sit on his ass back at the NDP. We not only moved on, we didn't stay long enough to destroy a section of the wires. I lost my pocket knife in Panama, and looked around for two small rocks to use to cut the wires – not a rock to be seen. We moved out, no time to waste.

I was sure that if a VC scout had been watching us from a vantage point, he would have been thinking 'What a bunch of fools'.

25

The incidents by the men, of hearing noises and seeing lights, disappeared with acclimation to the surroundings. Time passed slowly, but went without effort, thanks to the fact that squads caught so much ambush duty. Their nights out earned the whole platoon days off. We weren't used to so much time off, and the men had free time to sit around and bullshit, tell their own war stories, mark Xs on calendars, and reread letters from home numerous times.

We had a weapons test fire one afternoon, appreciated by the M-60 machine gun crew – always carrying around the heavy gun and two metal boxes of linked ammo, but seldom getting to use it. It was a morale boost for them to burn some ammo. Private Owens carried the M-60. He was a big, strong country boy from Missouri. One afternoon, I said, "Owens, I'm gonna make you my personal bodyguard, you big fucker. It's your job to not let anybody in the platoon hurt me. You hear?" He grinned a happy grin, and kept throwing the biggest Bowie knife I had ever seen at a tree. He threw hard, and it glanced away each throw. We were betting he would break the handles off before he ever got it to stick, as he bounced it off the tree, but they held; it was a knife of quality to take such punishment.

#

On patrol the week before we pulled out, we trailed the first platoon through some of the worst, thickest shit ever seen. I knew they couldn't see up front. Our visibility was less than ten feet to the flanks. I closed up our single-file formation, two or three meters between men instead of the standard five. The last man in line was responsible for watching the trampled path we left behind, turning around occasionally to make sure we had no VC stalking close behind. It wasn't normal to move jammed-up tight, but snaking along we maintained visual contact with the man to the front.

I don't know what went through the captain's mind, but he radioed back, "November 6, this is Delta 6 - Do you have flank security out?"

I typically talked to myself first when he called on the radio, or to my radio operator, or to anybody standing close enough to the radio to hear me. "Flank out? Is he fucking crazy?" I took the radio. "That's a negative," unable to understand why he would think about some crazy shit like that. We were the rear platoon, and unable to see to either side in the thicket. "Who the hell does he think could be in this shit where you can't even walk?"

The very thought struck me as insane, no matter what the operating procedures were. Under normal, even semi-normal conditions, I would have men out as much as a hundred feet on both sides of the main formation. The idea of flank security is to prevent an ambush from the sides, but it was effective only if we could be seen by the enemy. It made no sense in practically zero visibility.

I should have told him they were out, and been done with it, but I didn't. I was still under the belief I should follow orders given, which he did. "Get them out," he said.

I radioed one of the squad leaders. "Get two flank men out." All we needed was somebody beside us, in close. I didn't elaborate. I was certain the flank men would be told to stay in visual contact or voice contact with the platoon, or no more than ten feet out. If they couldn't hear us over their own noise of thrashing around in the thicket, they could have veered toward the platoon at any time to catch sight. Maybe they weren't told. Sometimes common sense failed.

In less than thirty minutes, the right flank man opened up. It was Private Tibbs. He carried an M-14, loaded with 7.62mm. duplex rounds. They were special because each round carried two projectiles that separated a few inches after firing. He wanted to carry the heaviest rifle firepower he could. He wanted to look hardcore.

Up front, men were screaming. "Medic! Medic! Cease fire! Medic!" The company had made a turn to the right at a checkpoint, the noise going across the front of Tibbs who fired with his M-14 on full automatic. The location of the burst sounded like Tibbs had wandered way the fuck out of position, too far out and too far forward of our platoon.

Sergeant Okemah, Platoon Sergeant of the first platoon, was on the ground. He didn't survive. He was an American Indian with nineteen and a half years of service and could have retired upon his return to the States. I knew him only to speak to around the NDP. He always looked old to me – he was thirty-seven; a twenty-five-year-old looked old to me. My own Platoon Sergeant, Sergeant Miyamoto, also had a lot of years of service. It was the unwritten practice that the older platoon sergeants stayed near the rear of the platoon where travel was easier and further away from initial contact in firefights, normally a safer place. In part, it was respect for their number of years in service.

I had too much anger over the incident to sit down and talk to Tibbs. Any soothing words about what he did would have to come from another source. He was visibly shaken from the first minute and would suffer the worst kind of scar for the rest of his life – the weight of guilt. The next morning, Private Tibbs got on a helicopter, either to a job in the rear or assigned to another unit. There were no good-byes from the men.

Tibbs was in the platoon when I arrived and had as much time in the field as myself. He acted like any other man around the NDP, never showing any nervousness. I asked his squad leader if maybe Tibbs was a mental case before then. He thought he was okay; he talked and joked like everyone else, looked like everybody else.

Sergeant Okemah's gear would be returned to the supply room to wait for the next man. His rucksack was lighter, gone was the weight of hope, dreams, plans for the future that he carried wherever he went. I thought about Sergeant Okemah's family that night, maybe even prayed for them. I could not have felt worse as I envisioned them receiving the news of a non-combat casualty. What kind of unanswered questions would they have? War has no compassion.

26

On the morning of the fourteenth day, several hundred men of the 1st Battalion packed up, emptied sandbags back into the holes dug the first day, rolled and tied them on their rucksacks. I hated the place from first sight, so it was good fucking riddance.

The two previous weeks had been a goddamn piss-poor adventure, if not downright disastrous. Enemy body count – zero; Platoon Sergeants killed by friendly fire - one, tracker dogs killed by incoming rounds - one. Yes sir, it was a hell of an operation. The only good part was fourteen more Xs on my calendar with the picture of Jesus on the back, fourteen days closer to home; the thought of a half-month was good. Sometimes I would wait a few days to mark them, just so I could put several Xs at once. It made no difference, of course. A day was a day, but it was the simple psychological pleasure of erasing several days of my remaining time there at once.

There was no chopper ride out of that shit hole. We went out on an Eagle Flight, a serious misnomer. In truth, it was a fucking three-day hump through whatever our compass azimuth took us through. We were loaded with full field gear, rucksacks packed with our worldly possessions, and a roll of ten or twelve dirty sandbags.

I figured the Colonel had planned the walk-out to extend his singular ground experience as Battalion Commander by actually walking on the ground, something he had never done. So, we humped. It would give him something to talk about; you know - create fucking memories. I considered him a politician, making himself look good, doing shit nobody needed. I never felt like he was the type that would do what he asked others to do, contrary to what was expected of good officers.

Nobody in our company liked him. He always flew around in his small observation chopper, making a nuisance out of himself, directing something from the air that didn't need directing. He must have thought things looked the same at ground level as they did from a few hundred feet up. The running joke in the company was that the only reason he wasn't shot down by friendly fire was out of consideration for his pilot.

#

The first day the battalion moved three hundred meters, stopped, circled into defensive positions and dug in for the night.

The second day, Delta Company had point for the battalion and my platoon's fate put us on point for the company. It was much like the day we arrived, when it took forty-five minutes to move six hundred meters. Our luck ran out at the worst time when it came to terrain; that morning was second to none when it came to bad. Carrying everything we owned on our backs was pouring salt in the wound. Brush and vine thickets rose out of the ground like woody tentacles, grabbing, pulling, tripping every man that dared trespass.

It took elbows, shoulders and feet in whatever manner, snatching and twisting our way, pushing and staggering forward, foot by foot at times. The struggle was amplified by all the weight strapped on from the waist up, raising our center of gravity, working the legs to maintain balance.

Palmer was our point man and had the worst job of all. He not only had to bust through the shit, but watch for gooks too, but he liked it up front. He looked like a beach boy, blond hair, nice smile, kind of an angelic, handsome bastard, but deadly tough.

#

The compass man walked behind the point to keep us on course. There was an unwritten set of rules for the point and compass men, especially in rough going. Every man in the field knew that it was impractical to try to walk in a straight line in such shit, so the point would weave our way through the least resistance.

There was no secret about it, just common sense. Given a choice, he knew the best direction to change. If checkpoint C was to the right of checkpoint B, then the worst pockets were circled to the right, eventually putting us to the right of checkpoint B. That made the distance to C shorter and so it went from checkpoint to checkpoint during the day. The compass man would shave a few degrees off the course to our advantage, shortening the distance to next check point maybe two hundred meters. It was no more than cutting across a corner, rather than walking all the way around it. Time was saved, and everybody was happy if it made our day end a few minutes early. Grunts were a bunch of pragmatic bastards, if nothing else.

Our dipshit company commander never questioned the compass heading, but the battalion REMFs walking in the back neither knew nor understood walking up front. The colonel was strolling down a garden path mashed down by a couple of hundred men. The path was perfectly flat I am sure, as he practiced his map reading and compass skills.

He noticed our azimuth discrepancies, called the captain on the battalion radio, who would relay the message to me on the company radio to get back on course. "Fuck you. You come up and stay on course," was my off-radio reply. It happened two or three times that morning; I paid little attention to the ignorant from the back of the formation. Up front, we had already begun to rotate the point man every few minutes due to fucking exhaustion. We were busting our asses trying to keep moving and had a goddamn clueless backseat driver complaining, the same way that things always looked so simple from his helicopter.

Noon came and went without a break to stop and eat our C's. I radioed back. "Delta 6, this is November 6, over."

"November 6, this is Delta 6 Kilo, over." Kilo was the RTO and he always answered.

"Roger, 6 Kilo. We need a break up here to eat - wanted to know when we are going to stop and eat - Over."

"November 6, Delta 6 Kilo - Wait one." The request was relayed back to battalion.

The return message: "November 6, Delta 6 Kilo."

"Roger, 6 Kilo, November 6." We abbreviated radio procedures to the minimum.

"Yeah, Roger, that's a negative on stopping. Dogface 6 has already eaten; said they were standing still back there. He said 'Get back on course and stay there.' 6 Kilo, out."

Dogface 6 was the battalion commander's call sign. 'What useless fucking bastards!' I turned to a boil inside, not for myself, but the lead squad, probably the only ones in the battalion who had not eaten, or even had a rest break all morning.

I stayed off the radio, worked my way by a few men to the front, to relay the command sentiments. I told Palmer, "Whatever you do, do not get off course again for anything."

Later, Palmer came to a dead stop, and relayed back that I needed to come up and look at something. I made my way forward and stood in front of a massive wall of fucking solid, impregnable vegetation. It went up, left and right, and nobody was going to walk through. Machetes wouldn't have gotten up through it.

"You want me to go around?" was his question. We could have gone off course, circled a long way around, and have the assholes on the radio again. I was looking for an answer, thinking, when my eyes dropped to the ground, at the base of the mess. It wasn't as bad at ground level, where there were two or three feet before the twining entanglements began. A light bulb went off. I was no longer concerned with the misery, or anything else.

My thinking was different than Palmer's practical approach. Still pissed-off about the no lunch break and wandering off course complaints, my prayer was answered; it was the place for revenge. I had the world right where I wanted it.

"Hell no. We'll go through it," I said. On hands and knees, shit strapped, hanging and dragging behind, we burrowed through to the other side. I sent my own message about what it was like to go straight. We left a tunnel of fifty feet or more, hoping every son-of-a-bitch in the battalion had to crawl through. It made me smile, visualizing battalion headquarters fuckers crawling on all fours.

27

Clear of the walled thicket, the day gradually became navigation friendly. Entanglements of vines gave way to merely thick bush, a monumental relief to not have everything from boots to weapons hanging up on vines. The radio was quiet with no more calls about going straight.

We were moving at a slow, constant pace when Palmer walked upon a single VC. He tried to open fire with his M-14, but only one round fired. A dented magazine caused a jam. It was the second time it happened to him; the first time was when he triggered our ambush about a month earlier.

The VC took off running. I radioed back to our CO, who in turn radioed battalion headquarters. They neither wanted us to pursue, nor to spread out and sweep the area. "Move on" was the command. Maybe they looked at their watches, deciding we were behind schedule, or they were bored and didn't want to stop. Who the hell knew what they were thinking, but it wasn't a rat's ass concern that we could have been walking into an enemy base camp.

'Always move on. Dumb fuckers!' I was beginning to think maybe Broos may have been on to something with his motto; 'The higher they get, the dumber they get.'

Visibility was poor. Palmer was the only one who caught sight of VC, but we knew one man wasn't going to be out in the bush alone. He ran off wearing only one Ho Chi Minh sandal; Palmer scared him out of the other one, a souvenir of the day. All we could do was pass the word, up the adrenalin a notch and keep our eyes open, hoping he didn't have a lot of friends nearby.

Before we resumed our regular pace, I did take time to impress on Palmer that if he wanted to live much longer, he'd better find some usable fucking magazines, and get rid of his dented shit. He may not be so lucky next time. Rummaging in his ammo bag, he found a good one and clicked it in. They were most likely dented by banging his rifle around to clear the way through vegetation. The year before my arrival, point men had the option to carry a 12-gauge pump shotgun loaded with 00 buckshot for in such conditions. A shotgun would have been handy that day.

Later in the afternoon, I received a radio message to hold up and stand aside. Charlie Company would be taking over point the remainder of the patrol. 'What the fuck is going on? Assholes back there complaining all fucking day until we shut them up with the crawl, travel finally becomes bearable, now somebody else is taking over? Maybe we pissed them off with the tunnel, so we were getting pulled.'

We'd been fighting a miserable and frustrating day. The heat, sweat, heavy load and aggravation of nature and command took its toll. A bit of paranoia crept into my thinking. The companies were merely realigning in the correct order for moving into our NDP that evening and out the next morning. At least that's what I believed once we got there and I could see where everyone was.

My platoon spread out on our flanks and provided security while Charlie Company filed through to the lead. We were probably less than two hours away from digging in our NDP. Sometime after taking over the point, they walked upon a cache of rice. It was estimated at two thousand pounds. I don't recall what they did, but they probably slashed the bags and slung the rice out in the bush; it was not left usable. Before reaching our NDP coordinates, they made contact and killed three or four VC and captured two rockets. I envied them for action that day, and was pissed off because of what we had gone through busting our ass up to the point of easy movement, then being replaced by them. It was the damn contact magnet again, typical that other companies seemed to find action and we miss it. Considering our company's leadership, maybe we were lucky.

We moved into our sector of the NDP. The area was covered by small trees, four to eight inches in diameter, raised canopies free of low hanging limbs, and clear of heavy undergrowth. By my standards it was like a park. When the perimeter was laid out, a bit of luck had my position fall right on a bomb crater, five or six feet deep and at least twice that in diameter. I was thankful for the readymade hole for the night, then Captain Dipshit came by and bumped our section of the perimeter outward so he could use it. I hoped the bastard would slide to the bottom and not be able to get out the next morning. We dug a shallow rectangle, large enough for myself, the RTO, and platoon medic to sleep, and filled a few sandbags, stacked two high to form a small shield to the front.

Charlie Company was linked to us on my immediate right. Their LP, stationed a few meters outside the perimeter, saw three VC as dark settled. They blew their claymores and had a short, fruitless firefight. It was probably a probe at Charlie's sector, in order to plot their exact location. It put us on full alert. There was nothing difficult about finding us; we left a flattened trail wide enough to drive a jeep through all the way back to Highway 13. My main concern was to cover the trail that night to keep anyone from using it to sneak up on us.

By 0600 hours the next morning, men were up from their sleeping positions, readjusting gear, dumping sandbags to roll and tie on, or eating C-rations, preparing to move out after sunrise. That was when incoming rounds landed directly on

Charlie Company. Several explosions jolted the whole area, one or more rounds must have struck a tree, scattering an air burst of shrapnel over their heads.

My position was little more than fifty meters away. I could see the commotion thru the trees. It was quick... then it was over. Some of my men rushed to get a report, see if it was anybody they knew. I chose not to go; there was nothing anybody else could do for them. It was better to stay clear of bad karma. I didn't need to see what happened, only know what happened. My men gave me a report.

I couldn't understand why Charlie Company was the chosen target, out of the whole battalion, but I suspected it may have been because of contact the afternoon before, or from the probe on their listening post. Maybe they were watched the entire time, visually followed to their positions in the NDP. Two were killed, eight wounded. Five of the casualties were in Lieutenant Mello's platoon. He was the one I arrived in country with on the same flight. I received word of his own death ten days later in a place called Song Be, near the Cambodian border.

Alpha Company took point on our delayed departure. It was the last day of the Eagle Flight. Once again, the point company made contact, had a body count of three, and found a large, empty base camp, including several tons of rice. It could well have been one of the staging areas for the Tet Offensive, or the expected counter-offensive. The cache required every man, including myself, to shoulder the burlap bags of rice from their storage to an open area for pick up by choppers.

The albatross still hung around our necks for unknown reasons when it came to even minimal action. I considered it bad luck on our part. We needed some kind of action with frequency to keep a mental edge which indirectly provided a morale boost, but it was needed mostly to relieve the tedium. Of course, we were spared from the early morning mortar rounds; maybe we couldn't have it both ways. Luck was a well-used word in the field for both good and bad.

#

Sprawled out at the PZ at 1700 hours, we listened for the reassuring, familiar sound of the Hueys. It was a good ride back.

When we set down on the chopper pad at Lai Khe, expectations were of a night in a bunk. Plans changed. We un-shouldered our rucksacks and dropped them on the floor of the barrack then straightaway, climbed on a truck for a night of berm guard duty.

While the trucks rolled around the long string of remote bunkers, it rained for the first time since I had been in-country. It was a sign of coming change. Nobody who had been around for months spoke well of the wet season. I thought I would like it, but I quickly understood the other point of view after leaving the truck.

The bunker's interior was covered with wet, gritty clay. Ground to a powder during the hot, dry season, it was already damp, sticking to my wet plastic poncho every spot it touched. The inside of my poncho was soon covered with wet dirt as much as the outside, losing any value; it was no longer wearable. Rain seeped and crept into the bunker, ruining all usable horizontal space. Thoughts of lying down were gone; it was the first of many future nights of misery. I would learn soon enough about rain and being in the infantry.

A hot meal waited for us after daylight. After breakfast came clean clothes and a warm shower, precious mail and a day off. The village sang its siren's call for those with carnal needs, cold beer, or nothing better to do than wander around free, carrying no more than a rifle. I wanted nothing but a soft bunk and to stretch out with my fresh mail and clean stationery. Letters needed to be written and dry sleep to be had.

28

The full twenty-four hour rest in Lai Khe revived the platoon. A day earlier they were like wilted flowers. Spirits shot even higher when I brought briefing news of moving farther north up Highway 13. Our next home would be an artillery fire base named Caisson 6. It was one of several fire bases dotting the highway for miles to the north of Lai Khe.

The men who made the fire base rotations before chattered like excited kids at the words 'Caisson 6'. They were more than eager to share their knowledge and experiences about the good parts of Thunder Road, unlike the hell hole we just left. Some of them thought it was a reward to pull duty up on the road. As skeptical as I was that it was a benevolent act from higher-ups, it sounded good and I appreciated it all the same. The ground was high, dry, and shaded, exactly opposite of the rice paddies or the thickets we just left.

Loaded onto Hueys at 0730, we set course for a low, rounded hilltop a few kilometers south of An Loc. It was a pleasant ride, anticipating the move. I took my usual perch in the open doorway for a full view of below, all shades and textures of green, and no water in sight. The choppers followed the road most of the way as it formed a solitary red-brown line curving through the green landscape. The lack of traffic on the road made it picturesque from above. The only other man-made sight flown over was the lingering outline of an old, triangular French fortification. It was a reminder of impermanence, and I wondered what our own bases would look like someday. We, too, would eventually be gone.

Caisson 6's permanent residents were three or four 107mm. Howitzers plus a Duster with twin 40mm. Pom-Pom guns mounted on a tank chassis. It looked like a left over WWII weapon, but it was fierce, as I found out when they did an unannounced test fire one afternoon. I about jumped out of my skin.

Each artillery piece was enclosed by sand-bagged walls chest high, that were in turn encircled by infantry bunkers. An infantry company rotated security duty every two weeks. Outside our bunkers, the perimeter was formed of seven concentric circles of concertina wire stacked four or five feet high and laced throughout with trip flares. Not a blade of grass grew in the area.

A narrow road of crushed gravel circled between the gun pits and the rear of our bunkers. I understood why it was there the first time it rained and the packed, wet red clay became a skating rink. It was hard to walk on anything but the gravel.

My platoon faced the only long, open view beyond the perimeter, as the elevation gradually sloped away from our treeless sector. Thunder Road was on the opposite side of the perimeter, a short, steep downhill walk through the rubber trees.

As soon as we dropped our gear in the platoon's assigned sector, we performed the usual patrol. I looked forward to moving around in the old rubber plantation, to see if it was everything the men said. Sure enough, it was free of underbrush, dry, and all shade. I'd not even dreamed about a place where we could move so comfortably. We moved fast on the short patrol and were back in the perimeter by early afternoon. Used to three or four kilometers a day and returning exhausted, ten kilometers in the rubber made for a relaxed day. I never cared how long our patrol routes were.

Our accommodations were above previous standards. A table and seats had been cobbled together using wooden artillery ammo boxes. A cardboard checkerboard, peeling around the edges, with the flatness of a potato chip, was left on top of the table along with a few black and red poker chips.

It struck me one day that there was a noticeable lack of graffiti anywhere. The inhabitants of our bunkers changed every two weeks and no one had drawn on, carved or left messages that would tell who or what units preceded us – no names, no boasts, no insults, only empty bunkers and ammo box furniture. The checkerboard left behind even looked forlorn.

The single element of undeniable aggravation of the place was the red clay dirt. Dry or wet, it was ubiquitous and awful. Ground into fine powder when dry, it coated everything from hair to the sanguine-colored fingerprints on letters or trapped in the spine of my diary. Hueys leaving the chopper pad were invisible until they reached enough elevation to rise above the red cloak of dust. After a light rain, a two-pound pair of boots became five-pound weights; on patrol, I continuously kicked trees or used the butt of my rifle stock to knock the caked mud loose from my boots. The wet season was just starting up north.

Although the place was already to my liking, the first full day of operations showed why the old timers of the platoon looked forward to our assignment. We formed on the road at 0700 with minesweepers; one platoon swept north, the other south, clearing their segments of the road for convoy traffic. The other platoon had patrol, which rotated daily, so we had two days of sweeps and patrol every third day.

The highway had little traffic to disturb the choking dust. Maybe an old beat-up Vietnamese bus, a bicycle or two that

Stephen L. Park

braved the rock-strewn surface, and a late afternoon military convoy hauling supplies north. Despite the name Highway 13, it was a wide single lane, right down the center, and the larger traffic had right of way.

By 0900, the mine sweeps were completed, and two-man positions were posted every hundred meters, alternating sides of the road in a zigzag pattern. They were the road security throughout the day. That was it – sit, talk, or sleep as long as one man stayed alert.

Our security positions were no secret. The first day, small kids who couldn't have been more than ten years old worked their way from one position to the next along the treed hillside. They hawked hot beer, hot Cokes at three times our usual cost, and other comfort items. They spoke all the English they needed for their jobs, and were impossible to shoo away so I succumbed and picked through the wares of one of their top salesmen.

I chose a nice purple, plastic mesh hammock, the most subdued of the garish colors the kid had. Camouflage it was not. It was made for someone about a foot shorter than myself, but within minutes it was strung up between two trees allowing me to get a few inches off the ground and gently swing the day away. My radio was propped up against the tree within hands reach, for any messages, and I gave Keller the day off; he had to lie on the ground as he had declined to purchase such luxury as I had.

29

It didn't take much effort to get into the swing of things; I welcomed the relaxed boredom with open arms. Daily instructions for road security were simple – make sure one man is alert and eyes watching.

Patrols were easy, and sometimes a nice break from sitting in one spot for road security all day. I never tired of the rubber plantations, the relative coolness of the shade, the visibility, and the linear symmetry of the trees. In a perfect collaboration between man and nature, they were planted in straight lines, to the front, sides, or diagonally, any direction one looked. Whether the men in the platoon ever saw more than simply trees I didn't know, but the beauty and perfect order around me was relaxing.

#

The CO was up to his old standards. I spotted him one morning from my hillside position, coming down the road in the Jeep. I wondered why the hell he thought he was serving some purpose when he would ride up and down the road after we had swept for mines and moved into the trees.

I lay about fifty meters on the uphill side of the road. He reached for his radio handset the same time he passed directly below. He looked up and saw our position, but I didn't know if he recognized me at that distance. We weren't concealed, nor needed to be. I was reclined in the best comfort I could gain in my undersized hammock, strung high enough to get my rear end a foot off the ground. It was straddled by my legs, with both feet flat on the ground.

It began. "November 6 this is Delta 6, over." The radio was leaning against the tree next to my head, the corded handset on my chest. They rolled past our location.

"What the shit does he want now?" I asked before I squeezed the transmit button, "Roger Delta 6, this is November 6, over," I replied in bored slowness.

"Roger - you have a man in a hammock on one of your positions..." and ordered that I go ferret out the culprit and put an end to whatever his imagined infraction was. My brain did a quick whirl trying to think what kind of regulation might be against a minimal level of comfort, or use of purple in the field.

My training had always considered field expedience and initiative as positive traits, both of which I deemed myself as displaying. I wasn't sure what kind of training he had, but it sounded like excessive marching around on a parade field.

"Roger," I said, "I'll get out and find it," as if I would walk up and down both sides of the road looking for a hammock, should it have been someone else using one.

"Delta 6 - Roger out." 'The dumb ass had made his command decision for the day.

I slumped back, unsure of the difference between lying on the ground, using ammo bags and a steel pot as a pillow, and lying in a plastic hammock, other than one was comfortable, one wasn't. Unamused by the incident, I wondered what he could be thinking and discussed such stupidity with Keller to help pass the time. Keller wasn't much of a conversationalist and only listened while I discussed the stupidity part.

The day we left the NDP I rolled the hammock and tucked it inside the bunker with a note; I couldn't use it anywhere else. It was something I could leave for one lucky man in the next unit, a sign that someone else had been there.

#

We had only one company-size patrol in two weeks at the fire base. It went through the rubber plantation, a walking picnic. We trailed behind the second platoon, over the easiest traveling ground I had seen. Small weeds hardly grew in the dappled sunlight under the trees. Quietly traversing lightly-rolling terrain through the cultivated trees, we were well spread, five meters between men, two columns with ten meters between.

Each tree had a wire bracket attached that held a small, salad-size clay bowl to catch the dripping sap once the old spirals in the bark were newly scored. The bowls were in place, but it didn't look like the trees had been worked in a long time. All that was missing were a few old, rusty signs nailed to the trees announcing *Property of Michelin Rubber*, in French of course, but there were no signs. There were no more French either.

Our single form of entertainment on patrol was listening to radio chatter, but it had hardly broken the silence for most of the day. The quiet monotony was interrupted in the afternoon when Lieutenant Moore, call sign Mike 6, called back to the captain.

"Delta 6, Mike 6 - over."

The company came to a halt. Stops were a good time to shift gear straps to a different spot on the shoulders, adjust the load, maybe fire up a smoke and relax a minute while we waited on the holdup.

The captain acknowledged, "Mike 6, this is Delta 6 - over."

The instant I heard the crackle of squelch broken on the radio, I moved closer to Keller to listen to what was happening. Considering our surroundings that day, radio volume was turned higher than normal.

Mike 6 says, "Roger. We've found a five-hundred pound bomb up here - over." Everyone who could get close to a radio was checking out the transmissions.

The captain asked the most mindless, dumbest question possible. "Is it one of ours?"

I asked myself, "Jesus, where has this man been? Who the fuck does he think it could belong to?" It would have been a funny joke on his part, but he wasn't joking.

Subdued caustic laughter began by those standing close to squad radios, waving others in closer to relay the conversation. A company commander who would ask such a stupid question about an obvious situation was beyond foolish.

In serious calm, Mike 6 replied, "Wait one - let me check." He started with the color description and read everything word the bomb, into his radio. "It's OD (olive drab) in color with yellow markings, stenciled U.S. Ordnance, net weight 375 pounds..." on to the lot number and part number designations. The entire reading took twenty or thirty seconds. Then he said, "Roger, I think it's one of ours," with dry, slight sarcasm in his voice.

The muffled, low laughter around the radios built louder as he read, finally erupting into an uproarious howl nobody could hold in at the end of his message. I was bent over from laughing so hard. Had I been able to look up, I think I would have seen the leaves shaking on the trees from the noise.

It was the loudest and longest laughter I heard in an entire year. War was such, too few times.

We changed course, around the bomb.

#

Our patrol took us across Highway 13 one morning, into new areas. Only the west side was rubber plantations. The east side of the road was in a heavier forested area of undulating terrain with light undergrowth. It was enough to make us tune our senses higher than most days, yet travel was still easy enough at a good pace.

By early afternoon we were moving parallel to the highway and came upon a large clearing on the edge of the tree line. Beyond the tree line, everything was clear-cut on either side of Highway 13 for about fifty meters. The clearing was large enough for the platoon to spread out. It was a perfect time and place to get mis-oriented for part of the afternoon.

Units could and did get lost if they had leaders who couldn't read a map, but at other times it meant pretend to be lost; that was our case. In such instances, mis-oriented became an excuse if found in the wrong place; best to say 'I guess we got mis-oriented'.

I learned of the unwritten procedure from Lieutenant Brav, my predecessor with the platoon; he kept a thick paperback for such times. Although infrequent, I considered the short periods of down time a morale boost for the men. It was one of so very few perks for grunts – to find a comfortable place to just sit and do nothing.

I ordered security posted around the area, marked our location on the map and made a time check. Each thirty minutes, I would put a new dot indicating about where we should be along our route, if we were moving. From time to time during the day, I had to radio our location to the company CP using coded map coordinates.

After some time, one of the security outposts spotted a single truck and accompanying plume of dust coming our way. Somebody made it out to be a three-quarter ton box truck and within seconds one of the men jumped up, yelled "It's refrigerated." He took off at full speed toward the road, waving his arms to flag it down.

I asked, "What the hell is he doing?"

After the truck hauled down to a stop, a few more of us followed him out to investigate.

He explained later, he had seen one stop in a fire base one time and knew something good was onboard. Sure enough, the driver climbed out, opened the back door and started tossing out half-gallon cartons of ice cream until we told him to stop. He cared less, glad to know there were unseen soldiers along the road; it made him feel safer making deliveries alone.

We returned to our clearing and made distributions to an all-you-can-eat ice cream afternoon. There were two small problems. It started melting fast, and we had no practical eating instruments. Pockets were searched for anything useful. Flaps torn from the cardboard cartons were used to dig out our treats. I found out I couldn't eat a half-gallon of ice cream in one sitting, nor could anyone else. Stuffed, we had to toss the remains.

One rare benefit of the fire base assignment was that our mess sergeant and cooks traveled with the company. It meant two hot meals a day. The same truck had stopped at our mess tent on his route down the road.

Upon our return to the firebase, not a word was mentioned about our afternoon, and not one man took ice cream for dessert that evening. I feigned my fullness from the meal. The mess sergeant, in a half-state of shock, was scratching his head and cursing when no one wanted ice cream for dessert. Without refrigeration, he had to tell the cooks to throw out all that was leftover.

#

I got a message one afternoon. "Don't go to the company CP tonight."

"Hell, I've never been there at night. Why would I do that?"

"Well, somebody told me to tell you, don't go for any reason tonight. He's going to get smoked."

I asked only one question, "What about, Dude?" He was the captain's RTO and a former member of my platoon, our inside man for any useful information passing through company headquarters.

"He knows to sit by the exit."

I wanted to know no more. Later in the evening somebody from one of the other platoons pitched a smoke grenade in the captain's bunker; it was a small message of his popularity. The captain never mentioned it.

#

The Howitzer's fire missions usually started about the time we settled in for sleep. The ground vibration from the guns wrecked havoc on some of the men, causing diarrhea, but I didn't share their affliction; my stomach was made of cast iron when it came to food or external influences. My defense against the guns was cigarette filters twisted and stuck in my ears to ease most of the nuisance of the firing less than fifty feet away.

#

A star cluster flare was used to signal the time to leave the road in the afternoons. The flare was a short aluminum tube, the equivalent of handheld 12-gauge shotgun barrel. The butt end was slammed against the ground to fire and the flares left with a loud swish sound and exploded into a star burst much like holiday fireworks.

I sent the first flare toward a position across the highway, then positions on down fired theirs in succession, zigzagging along the road when they saw others. Everyone knew it was time to move. One day I sat spread legged and fired the evening signal. I missed the angle and they hit a tree limb about ten feet above and fell straight down between my boots. A short scramble ensued.

Another day, a late convoy was passing at the time for us to clear out. The last vehicle was a quad .50-caliber mounted gun, a serious piece of equipment. The gunner was leaned back and relaxed, probably tired of eating dust all the way up Thunder Road. I fired a low flat trajectory flare across the road just before he cleared my position. He jumped like hell when the sound went over his head. No doubt he would have loved to use that gun on me, but fortunately we were hidden and he was too slow.

#

I sat on the low roof of my bunker one night with the starlight scope. Staring into open darkness was my last resort to relieve boredom. I was studying the range and clarity of some landmarks I already knew from daytime mental notes. As I scanned side-to-side, I was stunned when I slowly swung through the concertina and spotted a big cat inside the wire. In disbelief, I took the scope away from my eye, unable see anything in the darkness, then quickly put it back to my eye. I'd not seen or heard so much as a bird since my arrival in-country; suddenly a huge cat appeared from nowhere, not fifty meters away.

Its head dropped, nearly touching the ground as he moved forward before it rose, followed by shoulders and back, as the form slunk under one wire, up and back down under another, repeating the wave-like motion moving parallel to our bunkers.

The wire did not appear in the scope, and it was impossible to know which set of rings it was moving through; I guessed about mid-way. The scope showed only the grainy, solid green form and I had no idea what big cats inhabited Vietnam. Judging the size slipping through the wire, it appeared to be low, panther-like, too small for an adult tiger, I thought.

I matched its silence; its head never turned to look the direction of our bunkers. I didn't say anything to anyone, unwilling to share the amazement of something so large, able to live undetected in the conditions of war. I could not imagine how a food supply existed for survival, wondering if the smell of garbage or humans brought it in so close.

Nonchalantly, I moved along our perimeter, from bunker to bunker with the scope, to the end of my platoon's sector. I worried that it would trip one of the flares wired into the concertina and some idiot would open fire. The cat's stealth and experience won out; I returned to my bunker and listened, hoping to hear complete silence, which meant life for the cat.

I sat on the bunker every night afterward, watching, but never saw it again.

#

The second week there, I got word in mail from Sherry that a classmate from Benning, Jack Brady, had been killed.

Our Battalion S-3, Operations Officer was killed during a low level, air recon flight by ground fire. It went through the floor of the small chopper, and he died before the chopper could get back to help.

The last was Mello, who I arrived in country with. We shared the battalion size NDP little more than a week before they moved north, near the Cambodian border, to Song Be. 'Whoever heard of Song Be?' I thought, 'What a fucking place to die - oh, he died in Song Be,' visualizing his body zipped up in a plastic bag to go back home. I hated the thought of dying in some shit place that couldn't even be found on a map.

#

By day fourteen, the rains were an expected occurrence in late afternoons or nights. The only exception hit at daybreak one morning at breakfast. I stood with my food tray tipped at an angle, draining water as I ate. Standing in the open was the only place to eat. The rain was an omen for the next four months; hardly a day went by without being wet from one thing or another.

#

While at our security positions, we were called in at 1300 hours without notice, as always, and were in Lai Khe by 1700. Our 'vacation' was over. It felt good to wash off the red earth; either as dust or mud it had bonded to everything we had.

30

We had received wrong information about our patrol. According to my briefing, one-third of the length was supposed to be through rubber trees. It became a five-hour race through six-and-a-half kilometers of crap to reach the PZ on time.

The choppers were late picking us up, we hit the LZ late, and terrain was the same as what we encountered a few weeks earlier; massive, thick underbrush of vines, briars, and red ants. Every step was slowed, and point men swapped out twice due to exhaustion of pace and conditions. As soon as we cleared the LZ, I already knew something wasn't right.

"Goddamn it, who in the hell drew up this shit on the map? Those fucking people at battalion need to know where the fuck they are sending us. If we don't get out of this shit soon, it'll beat our ass today." I had to verbally let the men know I understood and shared their thoughts, hoping to absorb some of their anger about the day. I had forgotten the battalion operations officer was killed a few days earlier, but that was no reason for such a screw-up by his replacement.

VC were not on our minds. If we couldn't operate in that terrain, neither could they. I focused on moving as fast as we could, and there was never any place we could move quickly. I had all the shit I was going to take before we reached the last leg of patrol. I stopped for a few minutes to study the map. It was time to look at the distance remaining and our rendezvous time for the choppers. We were short on time.

"Fuck this, take fifty degrees off the azimuth, we'll take out the last checkpoint and save a few hundred meters. We can pick up our last heading not far from the PZ." Two or three hundred meters would equate to about thirty minutes of precious time.

By the time the CO realized we were so far off our course, it was too late for a meaningful correction. We were already getting close to our destination. The dumb-ass should have been happy somebody was keeping up with the day. He must have believed the choppers would sit and wait if we weren't there for pick up. A no-show at the PZ and we could have been left out for an impromptu ambush. It was back to the same old crap; a captain who couldn't take enough initiative to get us out of a simple problem.

We would have been as well off if we had stayed in the bush all night; we got back in time for berm guard. We loaded into the back of open two-and-a half-ton trucks for an unbelievably long trip around the desolate berm; it rained. The two items taken to combat the elements, a poncho and air mattress were completely wet before we could unload and became coated with the sandy grit once inside the bunker. Thoroughly soaked before dark insured we would stay that way until the next morning, and it was a cold, miserable, dick-shriveling, pitch-black wetness for ten hours.

#

I was ready for something decent to happen; shit on top of shit got old. We had the day off to get ready for a company-sized ambush that night. The Lai Khe area fast lost its attraction. I became apprehensive of every area and operation.

After the company briefing, I passed on the information to the squad leaders to mark the coordinates on their maps. Two water crossings were between us and the ambush site – so much for hope of a dry night.

It got quiet. Eyes bore down on the map; a couple of sergeants familiar with the area had wheels turning in their heads.

"Yeah - yeah, I know where this is! Don't you remember? We were over in here one time." Sergeant Dennis was talking to one of the other old timers. After studying the map for a minute, he laughed.

"You know what's here don't you? You remember?"

Dennis turned to me. "Oh, you're not going to believe this place." Others were catching on to what he was talking about and started to laugh.

"Okay, I take it's not a bad area we're going into tonight." I was thinking they wouldn't laugh if it had a spooky feel. Sometime we would have 'feelings' about places that were nothing, except psychological.

"No, no it's not bad. The whole area is open, lots of visibility, but that's not it. You'll just have to wait. You're going to love this."

They couldn't keep the secret all afternoon. "Okay, I'll tell you. We're going out to where the 'fuck you' lizards are." Every time somebody imitated one, they laughed, still saying to me, "You just wait, you not gonna believe 'em. Those things are hilarious." The ambush had become secondary to the importance of a nocturnal field trip to find the lizards.

There was no rain, but no matter; the waist-deep streams had done their jobs and assured us of another wet night. It was hard to complain about the streams; ground water was a hell of a lot warmer than night rain.

In the last minutes of visibility, the platoon scuttled into our rear security positions behind a low, natural ridge not two feet high extending out from the wood line. We were lying in an open field. I was surprised how huge and open the area was, like nothing I had seen up there. The claymores were set out, but useless – nothing but wide, open space was within their range.

After full darkness set in, the lizards started. I could hear the men to either side straining muffled laughs. Dennis was right. It was a high-pitched sound taunting us from the grassy field. I grabbed the starlight scope to make sure nobody was there; the 'fuk yooouuuu' was so real, drawing out like a dog's howl in the distance. The sounds came from all over the open field and were truly hilarious; thankfully they didn't last all night.

Later in the night, another sound I never heard before faintly rolled in from far off. There was no mistaking cluster-bombs exploding, falling from high, never heard B-52s. The erratic pounding of the bomblets seemed to last for minutes, distant kettle drums beaten by imagined ogres.

#

The platoon had the next day off duty, but was on call as a RRF (Ready Reserve Force). The men were free to roam around the village but stay in groups able to hear the yell in the village. At 1500 hours, the "Delta company - saddle up." call came. The wandering men hustled back, geared up and were on the pad before the choppers arrived. There were no slackers. The briefing was hasty. We had insertion on the LZ.

Another outfit was already on the ground out there, somewhere. Our mission was to provide a blocking force to cut off enemy exit routes, to close the back door.

Our lead flight of Hueys had to make an extra pass over the LZ while a Cobra gunship escort made a rocket run, ripping into a nearby tree line. I didn't like to be in the air any longer than necessary, especially going in first. I hated to think we needed coverage like that; it raised the pucker factor by multiples. I told myself it was a pre-emptive precaution only. I never knew what messages chopper crews were sending or receiving. I never once used a radio while on choppers. I probably wouldn't hear it anyway because of the noise.

Our patrol moved five hundred meters without a dry step; we slipped through one stream, four feet wide and chest deep. Typical of the wet season, depth equaled or exceeded the width, and dry gullies in the mornings filled to capacity following afternoon rains.

The mission turned out to be a dry run.

#

I had seen Ben Cat on a map once, and heard the name mentioned as a place not to want to operate. I didn't know it was deep inside the Iron Triangle, where bad things happened.

Our Ben Cat operation was another first for me, an air assault combined into a two-company patrol. Maybe two companies were considered a safe size for the area; each one could act as support for the other if needed.

Alpha Company was the other part of the operation; later they split off and stayed out for ambush that night. Our first platoon, Lima, took point through partial rubber that turned into thick bush. My platoon moved along in the rear.

Just past noon, Lima's point man walked up on a base camp, about twenty feet in front of him, the limit of usable visibility. One man was hit twice and others caught shrapnel flying from our own artillery strikes.

The air was full of stuff flying, more than the usual contact, and every man was flat on the ground. It was hard to find enough cover in the brushy undergrowth to stop any low rounds, and too dense to see a damn thing. One of our fairly new men, Private Viehl, was on my right. I glanced over; he was poking his head up in a curious turtle position, his neck stretched out. There was nothing to be seen, nothing for us to do except wait. "Viehl, you might want to keep your head down right now," I told him in mock sarcasm. Later, I was sorry I didn't let him fill his curiosity for war. He had only three more weeks to live.

31

May 3 at Lai Khe was a state of confusion for our company. I received word we were moving to Quan Loi, a base a few miles north of DiAn. Most of the men were in the village on a little pre-departure free time. A call echoed through the village, thought to be an unexpected Reserve Force mission, for the platoon to report back. It wasn't. It was a change in destination, and we loaded on Chinooks for DiAn; it was good news to everyone. We were going home for the night.

We landed during a Yellow Alert for the base. There was no welcome home cook-out, no open officers club, no movies. Steel pots were worn at all times and weapons in hand. It was 1700 hours when we landed and curfew was at 1900.

Nobody knew the details of why the alert, only that the base had the big 122mm rockets incoming at times. It was a huge base and the rocket attacks usually targeted the chopper strip or ammo dump. It would have been damn nice if some specifics ever got filtered down to us.

Early curfew made for a good night to rest. I was briefed for the next morning's two-platoon patrol and would have the point platoon. It looked like a cake-walk, dry and flat. The rains hadn't yet arrived that far south.

We were geared-up and ready to head out of the wire at 0800 when the captain reversed the platoon order. No reason given, it was another arbitrary last minute whim of a decision the dumb prick was known to make. That sent Lima platoon out on point, just like that, out of the blue. My platoon briefing and subsequent planning down to squad level based on the previous night's briefing meant nothing. It made no difference to me about point.

Lima's platoon leader, Lieutenant Price, had been in-country about six weeks. We had talked briefly a couple of times about the usual things, home towns and wives. We were both from the same state. He was personable and likable, unlike his predecessor, a little rat-faced, lazy bastard I never liked. More important, his men liked him.

We filed through the north gate of DiAn, out across a dry, flat plain covered with sparse, waist-high scrub brush. Taking advantage of the coolest part of the day, we didn't stop for a break until 0930. Changing landscape left the low brush, and we began to weave around more impassable areas. The point made a ninety-degree right turn, then we filed along a scraggily tree line similar to an old farm fencerow overgrown with brush and saplings.

It was a quiet day with no radio chatter, just walking along, relieved to be away from the Lai Khe thickets.

There was an opening between the trees as we moved further down the line. The point man took a left to cut back and get on course. A clearing was on the other side of the trees, maybe thirty meters across and about the same in width. When I stepped through into the opening, I thought 'Why would the point cross an opening like this instead of following the tree line further around?' I was in the middle of the clearing when the firing started.

32

One man was in front of me; Spec.4 Reps from Colorado. My RTO was behind me as was the rest of the platoon. Reps ran forward, and I spun around to run back to the tree line. I didn't want to be separated from the platoon.

Tactically, I was in a bad place. I didn't know which direction Lima went beyond the clearing because of vegetation. It could have been left, right, or straight ahead. I couldn't see shit, not even Reps.

The sounds of the rifle fire didn't help; it was all at one or two o'clock from my position, and impossible to distinguish the well known popping sound of AK-47's from M-16's. I wanted to lay down fire to the right flank, but if the rear of Lima platoon had swung around to the right, it would be disastrous. I wouldn't risk shooting them in the back.

There were no radio transmissions. Within seconds, the CO was screaming on the radio, "November! Get up here."

I screamed back, "I don't know where you are...no visual. Pop smoke; mark your location! Pop smoke."

There was nothing; no smoke came up through the low canopy.

Each man carried two smoke grenades. Normally they were used to mark ground locations for choppers. In areas without good visibility 'pop smoke' was meant to let someone know your location. The color red was reserved to toss toward enemy positions.

Back on the radio, I called, "Any Lima kilo, pop smoke, anybody in Lima that can hear me, pop smoke so I can find you."

I wasn't going to flank the platoon across that much open space to the contact; we needed to lay down covering fire to get across the clearing. There were no radio responses, no smoke. It was fucked-up.

The captain was on his radio, still screaming, "November! - get your ass up here!" in pure panic. If he had been alone, I would have screamed, "Fuck you! Bastard, you got in it, you get out." Unfortunately he always had men in front of him to separate him from the shit. Those were the only radio messages he sent.

Reps popped back up from nowhere, running up the tree line from below us. "Those guys up there are in shit. They're getting cut up and need our help."

He didn't tell me anything I didn't know. "How did you get back to us?"

"Through a low place down by the edge of the clearing."

We were talking as fast as we could. "Can we get up there the same way you got back? How low is it?" I needed to be able to move the whole platoon through, not just a handful of us.

"I don't know if we can or not," he said.

I thought, 'Well goddamn, either we can, or we can't. What kind of fucking answer is 'I don't know'?"

By his description, I pictured a three or four-foot deep sunken area, not deep enough to safely move the platoon through.

The captain was still screaming everything except directing movement to organize the front of the patrol. I didn't waste time on him, I knew the son-of-a-bitch was down behind something and not going to move. He was no help, and I had no interest in personally saving his ass.

I had a choice of two directions. I knew if I went straight across I could find the back of the first platoon. The right edge of the clearing was maybe another thirty meters, about the same as the distance across. There was no visibility inside the wooded, dark shade. It was where the point man should have walked down to before crossing that open area, but he didn't. The other option was return however Reps got back. I didn't know what we would find once we came out on the other end, or where the other platoon may be.

We were in the only opening through the tree line and needed cover fire almost ninety degrees to our right; it was an impossible angle. I wanted the M-60 machine gun, but there wasn't even a vantage point for a rifleman. Goddamn I hated where we were. What a fucked-up situation. Just one weapon on the other side of the open field would allow an angle for covering fire back into the wood line. That would've given covering fire for the platoon to cross.

I knew the run across was stupid, but I couldn't ask anyone else to be first, and we had to move quickly. I glanced across the faces of Reps, Sergeant Dennis, and Keller. I didn't see any answers.

Normal senses shut off. Any fear was gone, and pumping adrenalin took over along with a clarity that it may be the last decision I would ever make. I put my chance of making it across no better than fifty-fifty, and there was nothing I could do to change it. In truth, I expected to die.

It had been two, three, four minutes it seemed, but I didn't know. A minute was forever in a firefight, and we walked into much more than a firefight.

I took a breath and moved out, bent over and too slow. There was no need to try to sprint with thirty pounds or more hanging on me. I made a few steps out when an explosion hit beside me. I was on the ground, not sure of how or why.

33

The VC did what I expected. One of them moved back in the woods to cover the rear. I was lucky he had an RPG instead of an automatic weapon.

My first thought, to lie still, lasted seconds. The number of thoughts that shot through my mind that went quicker than I would have believed possible; not the least was that I may be target practice for the next round. Every nerve and cell in my body was firing; I swung around on my stomach and without looking, low crawled as fast as I could.

Dennis, Reps, Keller, maybe somebody else was there. Sergeant Dennis was knocked to the ground by the explosion, but not hit. He was unbuttoning my shirt. I was telling him, "No, no, my hip bone, I need to check my hip."

I grabbed the thick pistol belt, gear, and pants, pulling everything open. Nothing, not a scratch on my hip bone from the powerful stinging seconds earlier. I couldn't understand but was glad, believing a piece of shrapnel or outer metal casing must have hit the belt flat; I didn't know, didn't care.

Dennis was still holding my shirt open. I asked, "What are you doing?"

"Watching for bubbles." A sign of a sucking chest wound, there were no bubbles. He yelled, "Somebody give me a bandage." I never felt anything hit my chest and couldn't see the clavicle area. Not that I didn't trust them, but I needed to see, to know for myself whether to be concerned or not. I couldn't understand why I didn't feel something.

They got a bandage tied on as best they could around my neck and chest, but it took time, something we didn't have. We needed to be moving. The captain kept calling, wanting somebody to get up there and save his ass. Dennis grabbed the radio. "November 6 is wounded." He told one of the men to take me back to where a Medevac chopper would land. I pulled off my ammo bags, water, grenades, and anything they needed to stay with the platoon.

I yelled up the line behind me for Sergeant Miyamoto, the Platoon Sergeant, to take over, but wasn't sure that was the right decision. I physically felt okay, in no pain, but mental confusion was going on about leaving the platoon. I didn't feel good about it, guilty if I didn't need to go, and not sure if it was needed or not.

I wasn't the first at the dust-off area and was unable to understand how anybody from Lima platoon could be there. 'How the hell did they get back here? How did they do it? Where did they come from?' It didn't make sense in my head, and added to the mental confusion. I thought, 'maybe I fucked up leaving.' There had to be another way to get to where Lima was if they made it back.

Lima 6, Lieutenant Price, was a few meters across the way, leaned back against something. One of his men sat beside him, crying. Two or three others were there, some dead, some alive I think, but I hardly noticed them. A medic was helping somebody. I wanted to scream for him to go over and take care of Price, but he wasn't moving. I guess I already knew; his color was gone. A pale gray form in jungle fatigues remained.

I sat, wanting to jump up and run back to find the platoon. I remembered I had given all my ammo away, and maybe they weren't in the same place anymore. I told myself they didn't need me. I felt like I had let them down even though they sent me away; I thought I shouldn't have been sitting there.

It couldn't have been five minutes before an APC rolled up out of the scrub brush and stopped next to the dust-off zone. Lieutenant Moore was the first to jump off the top. He had been our second platoon leader in Delta Company, left the field when his time was up then took over the Recon Platoon. They were a high-speed ground reinforcement for any units in contact. That day it was us.

I couldn't believe how quickly they got there, although we were only three kilometers from DiAn. Time had taken an abnormal perspective. It was a relief to see him. He walked to me and said, "Good job. We've got it."

I pointed. "November was just past there, in the tree line a few minutes ago."

I sat, waited and thought, slightly clearer of mind. Doubt set in. 'Could I have done something different? Better?' I had never thought of a situation where I would be separated from the platoon; it had a surreal feeling.

Flashes of home, almost subliminal, so quick, intermingled with thoughts. 'Where will I be this afternoon?' The picture of the clearing stayed in my head, looking at Price, images going backward to our goddamn company commander reversing our briefed orders that morning. I should have been on point.

34

The Medevac chopper didn't bring the relief I hoped for. I thought, 'If it was coming back later I could wait. Maybe I should just stay where I am.' In no hurry to climb aboard, I took my familiar seat on the floor, facing outward, legs crossed. The door slid shut. I sat facing the door.

After lift-off, the muffled, rhythmic sound from the rotors was all that was noticeable, but it didn't sound normal with side doors; I think the interior was padded. I'd never ridden on a Huey with doors.

Others were on-board, but I couldn't turn around to see who was dead or alive. I knew for sure Lieutenant Price was there. I was numb to everything except the muted sounds of the chopper, whop-whop-whop, thump-thump-thump of the rotors. Questions floated in my head along with thoughts of loosely related events. I focused on the rotors' sound, the only thing perfectly clear; I didn't want the chopper to land.

Inside the door of the 93rd Evacuation Hospital at Long Binh, I was told, "You can sit here. Somebody will get to you soon." A short row of folding metal chairs lined the wall. I sat on the end chair. I'd not spoken to anyone since I saw Lieutenant Moore.

People walked by, flipped through papers and talked quietly at a central nurses' station. I wanted to scream out, 'Across the river, people are killing each other,' but said nothing. It was like a stray bullet could almost reach the hospital; in their safety, they were unaware of the world I just left. I watched them move around. American females worked there. I hadn't seen one in awhile and couldn't help but stare, but they never noticed me in the chair. That was fine with me.

The change of my physical environment in minutes was bizarre. I moved between two completely different worlds, as easy as changing slides in a projector: there, here - here, there, see how simple. One life flashed off, another flashed on. It was so quiet sitting there.

Specialist Class 5 Washington walked up. "How you doing? Come on in here," he stepped into a doorway, "and we'll get you taken care of." I followed, without need to talk. Washington was huge, black, and talkative with an easy-going manner. "Lay back on the table there and I'll get you fixed right up."

The calm, quiet talk felt strange, like nothing else was going on in the world. My mind stayed with the platoon, wondering. I was sitting in two worlds at once, unsure of where I belonged.

"You're going to do it?" I asked, unthinking. An E-5 doing the work caught me by surprise; there were no E-5's in the platoon I would trust to do something like that. Of course they were all grunts.

"Yeah, it'll be okay. I do stuff like this all the time." He spoke with confidence.

He was determined to talk, and it gave me something new to focus on. A regular conversation was nice as he went about his business, but he did most of the talking. He got around to asking. "What happened?"

I told him that we went out on patrol and ran into some trouble. I didn't know that Lima platoon never saw the three- to four-hundred-man Viet Cong regiment in and around the village of Tan Hiep. Delta Company had stepped in deep shit, but I didn't know until later.

Washington produced a razor and a syringe of Novocain. Some light scalpel work, stitches, and he was finished in a few minutes. "There you go, my man; all done." He handed me a small piece of shrapnel.

I couldn't see his handiwork, but told him, "Thanks. Now how do I get out of here? Where do I go? If there's another Medevac going back out, I can ride back on it." I thought it would be simple to rejoin my platoon.

He told me "There will be no ride back today. Hold on a minute, let me find somebody," he said walking off. Five minutes later, he returned with a driver. "We'll get you over to 90th Replacement Company and you can catch a ride back to your unit."

The 90th was about the last place I wanted to be, but a short ride and I was back where I started seventy days earlier. It felt much longer than that. I was a different person; I lost the curiosity about war that I had upon arrival.

I walked into company headquarters, to the clerk's desk. "I just came from 93rd Evac and need to catch a ride back to First Infantry at DiAn."

He looked at the papers on his desk. "There's nothing going that way today, but maybe one tomorrow."

"OK, listen. You have a place in here where I can stow my rifle and gear? I don't want to drag this shit around with me."

The clerk noticed the rank pinned to the flap of my shirt pocket, rather than the customary collar location, and said, "Yes sir, it'll be safe in here. I'll take it, and if you'll wait a second I'll get you some clean sheets."

35

I walked along the row of wooden barracks, looking for emptiness. I found one with no signs of life inside, as far from the chatter and people milling around as I could get, and picked a bunk away from the front door.

I was exhausted. It had been a long day, but was only noon. I sat on the bunk, so good to be alone, away from everyone, no listening, no talking. I needed time to get thoughts sorted, and probably prayed to whoever would listen, for the safety of the men in the platoon.

I wondered what they were doing at that exact moment, each minute, if they had finished the firefight yet. I could almost hear it. Our position at the edge of the clearing was the main vision; I was unable to get it out of my head. When we stepped through the trees, I thought, 'We shouldn't be walking across this.' It just wasn't done.

I wondered about the experience of Lima's point man. Lieutenant Price hadn't been there long enough to know or catch the mistake. The goddamn company commander was walking along within their platoon; he should have known

147

better. He could've made a correction – stop and swing around the wood line, to do his job. You never walked across an open space enclosed by dense cover.

It wasn't even done in large, wide-open areas too far to walk around. The procedure was to stop and do what was called a weapons check, spray suspect woods with automatic weapon fire and drop in a few rounds from the M-79 grenade launcher. The area was then crossed with a much higher degree of confidence. Those situations were where an experienced, cautious point man or lead squad leader was a value.

In small areas, it was best to detour around, stay less visible and keep more cover. I believed part of the casualties hinged on crossing the clearing.

I had no doubt had we been up front, the point would have stayed with the trees, but too many 'ifs' swirled in my head that afternoon: if I had been left on point, as briefed, if I wasn't too relaxed after returning from Lai Khe the evening before, if we had reversed positions on patrol, would the results have been different, if we had a decent company commander less prone to fuck-up so much, if I had stayed with the platoon longer that morning, if the firing had started fifteen or thirty seconds later, able to see, to lay down fire. Maybe I would have made the same mistake. It was later when I found out there was nothing I could have done to save Lieutenant Price, his RTO or their other casualties. They were hit immediately.

I had to lie back on the bunk awhile, close my eyes and rest. That, too, was with guilt. The platoon wasn't resting.

The company area had an Officer's Club across the street from the Headquarters building, where incoming and outgoing could have a few drinks for different reasons. At dark, I went over in hope of finding someone fresh in from the division.

Through the front door, straight across the large room, I spotted two Big Red One shoulder patches at the bar. It was a subdued club, no loud or unruly noise even from those soon to depart. I walked directly over; the two standing at the bar were lieutenants.

"Hey, how you guys doing? Did you come down from DiAn this afternoon?"

They looked at me, unimpressed, possibly from my unkempt appearance. I looked the same as when we walked out of the wire that morning, maybe dirtier, certainly dirtier than any other person in the club. I didn't think about it, but I didn't care anyway; I wore dirt with pride.

As if it was a great effort to answer one fucking simple question, one of them said, "No, we're from Lai Khe." They worked in Division HQs. I paid no attention to what department or jobs they said, sounding like a couple of sorry-ass, privileged REMF's.

I looked around for other First Division patches in the room; I was stuck with those two for any information. "Did you by any chance hear of any action around DiAn today, with the First Battalion of the Eighteenth?"

"Yeah, we listened to it for a while on the radios in the operations center then had to leave about 1400 hours to catch the chopper to get here."

Listening from division headquarters, some sixty kilometers away surprised me. "Could you tell what was going on? Anything happening?"

"They were still engaged when we left." They had been listening to frequencies at battalion level, armored and air support units. They couldn't hear anything on company level radios.

Trying to pick as much information as I could, I asked about casualties. One said, "I believe two platoon leaders were KIA." My mind froze for an instant at that, speechless.

"No, no, that's not right," I told them. "I was out there. There were only two platoons."

They shrugged their shoulders. It added more questions and possibilities in my head. I'd wondered if maybe Lieutenant Moore, with the Recon Platoon, had been killed after he arrived. Did they mean I was reported KIA? Those were the only two choices imaginable, but they never mentioned WIA's. I couldn't make sense of what the hell was going on.

I returned to my bunk, drained. It was early and quiet, the building still empty. The clean, folded sheets lay on top of the limp, S-folded mattress. I didn't even unfold the mattress. I stretched out on the springs, using the mattress for a pillow, my boots hanging over the foot of the bed. I unbuttoned my shirt to cool a little. The bunk felt luxurious. I fell out until well past dawn.

36

I saw two sets of fatigues standing next to my bunk as I got my eyes open. I looked out from below the top bunk to say hello; they were two warrant officers, helicopter pilots, fresh from the States. They looked like I did ten weeks earlier, starched and creased pants, spit-shined boots. They were shiny all over.

Outside the end door of the barracks, the sun was high and bright by the time I woke. Late by military standards, the day had started for everyone except me; I was on my own time and breakfast would be a couple of Marlboros.

The building was empty except for the three of us, all around the two bunks. I thought that was a hell of a coincidence. They weren't doing anything. Their bunks were straight, nothing lying around. One was acting busy with his bag, the other started a conversation of sorts.

He explained. They came in the night before, saw me sleeping on the bunk springs, boots on, shirt open, a gauze square taped to my chest, and nothing around but a steel pot. When they woke up, I was in the exact same position.

I figured maybe they stopped back by out of curiosity, like gawking at a car wreck. I wasn't exactly presentable in a place like 90th Replacement. Unused to human kindness in recent times, I was wrong; they were simply and honestly concerned and patiently waited around until I woke. The one who began talking asked if they could help. I thanked them, explained how I got there, that I was waiting on transport back to my unit, and appreciated their concern, but I was okay.

Maybe he thought I hadn't looked in a mirror lately and offered his shaving kit: a razor, soap, shampoo, and a towel. I hadn't looked in a mirror, and the thought of cleaning up was irresistible; I gladly accepted and was off to find a shower. I thought better of chopper jockeys from then on; he was the kind of man you would want for a friend. I should've written his name down and given my name and APO address so I would know his location or unit. I was so groggy it never entered my mind, but it would have been extra baggage anyway. I traveled light and had few social skills.

A warm shower was far beyond refreshing for both body and mind. While shaving, a spot on the lower part of my neck started bleeding. "What a piece of crap razor this is," I said, inspecting the blade. I found a tiny piece of black shrapnel wedged beside the blade; it came out of my neck between the Adam's apple and carotid artery.

Redressing, I noticed my shirt had a fresh, finger-sized hole in the back. The edges of the threads hadn't frayed. A corresponding short scrape mark was below my right shoulder blade. That made me closely examine everything. The thick canvas, helmet cover also had a fresh rip, the green paint beneath had been removed down to shiny metal. I looked at my pistol belt before, but inspected it again, still nothing. I was amazed that the only place that stung like hell didn't have a mark, on it or me.

I sat on the wooden bench in the shower house. "I'm one lucky son-of-a-bitch," I told myself. Somehow I had squeezed between pieces of flying shrapnel; nothing was more unpredictable than shrapnel. A small piece hit my chest and scraped my back at the same time, the only sizable piece between them hit my helmet. I thought, 'What if he'd had an eighth-inch more elevation on the RPG launcher.' It was always luck, good or bad.

Thinking about the day before had to be pushed aside. Whatever happened was done, the company would be back in DiAn, and I would be back that afternoon for a detailed debriefing from my men.

What the two lieutenants had said in the bar about casualty reports, two platoon leaders were KIA, came back to me. I didn't know how the Army processed information, but I couldn't believe in its infallibility.

A local PX was a five minute walk. I needed a pen, writing tablet and envelopes and didn't want an unexpected mail delivery gap at home; my priority was to get a letter on the way that day.

Two letters were written. One was to Sherry, and one to friends who lived in the same apartment complex. Sherry's letter was a standard daily letter; where we were, what we were doing, and to say everything was going fine. The other was a brief recount of what happened, in case Army reporting got screwed up far enough down the line. I told them I was okay, but in case any bad news reached home, it was wrong, and they were to correct it. "P.S. Do not mention this letter to Sherry; she doesn't know."

I checked in with the company transportation clerk several times during the day. "Sorry, nothing today, probably tomorrow," was all he could say. Fresh letters were dropped in the mail bag.

37

After three days at the 90th Replacement Company, a truck from division came to pick up a handful of new troops. I hitched a ride to go home, hoping the men would be glad to see me. I didn't know the outcome of May 4, or how life had been since. Three days was a long time.

The men were still in DiAn and were off when I arrived because of ambush duty the night before. I was glad to see a few of them hanging around the company area. I was in dire need to be brought up to date. Some were surprised to see me. I hadn't thought about it, but they knew no more about me for three days than I did them. In the confusion of the day, my status was initially reported as possibly killed instead of wounded. My first question to them was, "Are you sure it was straightened out?" I thought back to what the two lieutenants at the bar said that night. I was glad I wrote an explanation to friends at home, to be on the safe side.

The battle on May 4 lasted nearly twelve hours, until 2200 hours. It was hard for me to believe how long the day had been for them. The fact that I missed eleven hours of it made me feel worse about my absence. The company was told that we caught the end of two VC battalions, and walked into an ambush. If true, it was no more than a hasty attempt at an ambush; otherwise, most of the company could have been wiped out. I didn't believe the ambush theory. The total Viet Cong. body count was two-hundred and thirty. That was all the men knew. Later intelligence reported a VC regiment was forced to spend two nights at their village, instead of one. Their guide failed to show up the night before to move them to another area. My men's voices held no jubilation from the day.

We had a memorial service for our casualties. The battalion commander made an appearance with words of praise and couldn't have been more pleased to announce the one-sided kill ratio. "We showed them," he said. "We lost a few men, but it was a great kill ratio; we should all be proud." I watched and listened. That was his thoughts on the day - a good kill ratio. The men sat stone-faced; nobody gave a shit about anything he said. Any memorializing carried out within the company was done on an individual basis. I wished I had talked more with Lieutenant Price, but nobody in the company dwelled on death. I imagined that inside they were glad it wasn't them. Everyone knew the next morning was a new day and the same old job.

I was placed on light duty until the stitches were removed. My return to full duty began with an ambush that night. The thought entered my mind a few days earlier, of whether or not I might be apprehensive about going back in the field. I wasn't. It was a comfort to be back with the platoon. The rest period was unimaginably refreshing, but I felt bad watching the men come and go on daily operations, especially the shit days or nights when they came in looking tired. There were times I stayed out of sight while they geared-up, slightly ashamed of my light duty due to no more than stitches.

My first night's ambush was followed by an Eagle Flight the next afternoon. It wasn't enough that I hated the three-day humps, but I was weak and dizzy when I got up on ambush. I was paying for the light duty, I thought. I'd gotten out of rhythm of life in the field. It sucked every ounce of effort inside me to pack my gear for three days. I couldn't walk straight. My mind worked in slow motion, physical movement even slower. I didn't make any unnecessary moves. Jesus, I wanted to say, "I'm sick and need a doctor. I can't go out." However, unless I was on the ground, or vomiting, or had similar symptoms worthy of medical help, doctors were only a thought. With everything I owned in the field hanging on me, I was close to involuntarily falling to the ground.

Small delays that slowed the day saved me. The choppers were late, I tried to sleep during the flight to the LZ, rest breaks, anything that kept me from walking helped. I asked the medic if he had any help in his bag. Relief came from 1200mg of Darvon capsules every couple of hours. It didn't take many to make me nonfunctional from Darvon. I hardly raised my eyes from Keller's boots in front of me, oblivious to everything. One foot dropped in front of the other as I wove and stumbled until after dark. A late day stream crossing fulfilled our unavoidable fate for a wet night.

Good fortune breathed on me the next morning. We packed up, moved a kilometer and stopped at a river. Far too wide for our standard hand-over-hand rope technique, we had a half-day of rest waiting for an engineer unit to arrive and assemble a mobile crossing platform. I lay in the shade gaining strength to finish the day.

Our night's ambush operation was aborted, and we were redirected to a rendezvous with Alpha and Bravo companies. Then mid-afternoon, an on-the-fly operational change to link up and create a three-company NDP for the night was destined to be a royal fuck-up. I cringed at the thought as soon as we got word. We didn't stop moving until 2200 hours. By then, I supposed the three company commanders were confident we were in positions that it would be difficult to shoot one another during the night. We were also soaked by rain. The assumption that we were in anything that resembled a three-hundred man circle formed in the dark was unlikely.

Minutes after daybreak, mortar rounds fell on a company area across the perimeter. The rounds were close enough to speed us up getting out of the area at first light; we didn't want to be part of a large target. The VC were better at knowing where we were than we them.

It was the last of the three days. I was recovered from whatever I had. Tired and ready to get the hell out of the boonies, the main thought in my head was the relief of the sound of Huey's coming toward us that afternoon. The point platoon made light contact once, without casualties on either side. There would be no chasing that day; we stayed on course toward our PZ destination.

We had the night off to dry out and sleep in a bunk then it began again the next evening at 1700 hours. That day gave time to receive mail, write letters, and mark my calendar with three more Xs. It finally began looking like a proper calendar, with more than two full months crossed off and a little wear around the edges.

The next day, we had an air assault out for ambush. In addition to regular gear, we carried rucksacks, two claymore mines per man, and the dreadful flak jackets were back with us.

38

We left the ambush site and patrolled the two-and-a half kilometers to our next NDP. The morning sun beat down, humidity was insufferable, and sweat rolled from every pore. Each man carried a minimum of sixty pounds, RTO's and machine gun crews more. We were little more than pack mules with our ruck sacks and flak jackets added to our regular gear. It was a good thing we never had contact under those conditions. Offensive maneuvers would have been next to impossible.

Our new NDP was a nondescript semi-flat field called the Peanut Patch. We decorated some villager's sprouting crop with bunker holes and surrounded it with concertina wire. The dry location was welcomed by the platoon. It was north of the river mud and south of the heavy, sticky red clay along Thunder Road. The monsoons were gathering into a seasonal pattern as months of dust and parched vegetation were gone. Green sprung up across the rolling hills. Patrols moved fast and easy, and large open spans reduced daylight hiding places for VC. It was a welcome change of locations.

The day after moving into the new NDP we were on a platoon-sized patrol. It was good to be away from the company after the last few days. Our patrol route took us across a wide, shallow valley. An oasis sat in the lowest part, a small island of green grass and palms amid rice paddies filled by the new rains.

We stopped for a longer than average break. With visibility at least a kilometer in any direction, it was a good place to become mis-orientated for awhile. The scene was a perfect idyllic cliché that made me forget about the war for awhile. We sat, cool and comfortable, under the shade of the high palm fronds. All that was missing were picnic blankets, potato salad and fried chicken. An old man plowed the paddy next to us. He moved behind his water buffalo and wood plow, tilling the packed mud bottom, back and forth from one dike to another. He was surefooted in the knee-deep water, and the animal slow and obedient. I watched the old man plow for over thirty minutes; he never once acknowledged our existence by looking our way.

#

Mosquitoes loved the new season, hungrier than ever. I hated mosquitoes. On ambush nights, I buttoned my shirt to the neck, sleeves were rolled down and cuffs buttoned. Repellent was rubbed on every square inch of exposed skin, including inside ears and on eyelids. The horrible, oily taste always managed to get on my lips, and I could hear their constant buzzing in my ears as they searched for that one unprotected spot of skin.

#

Routes taken across paddies of company-sized patrols were at the mercy of the point platoon's decision. Walking dikes were the dry and easy way to traverse, zigzagging atop the narrow earth barriers, continuously making ninety degree turns. The alternative was a straight line through the laborious mud and water. Crossing waist-high dikes required leaning over them and rotating on our stomachs to swing body and gear over. Whatever lived in the paddies during the dry season moved to the grassy dikes once the paddies were full of water. More than once, a Medevac was called to pick up a point man who took the sting of the large, crayfish-size black scorpion inhabitants of the dikes.

We stopped patrol one day to have a tracker-dog team dusted-off by Medevac. The German shepherd became exhausted as it struggled to navigate the muck for several hours. He didn't make it until noon. Of course, it was a ridiculous idea to send a dog on such a patrol. I never understood the logic behind sending a dog with a large portion of the patrol across rice paddies. It was in an absolutely useless area.

#

The CO halted our company patrol for a ten-minute rest break one morning. It wasn't a good place to stop, and nobody even sat down. We just stood in the open. He had a knack as the only man in the company who couldn't find a spot with minimal comfort for a break. Rain began while we stood. It never sprinkled or drizzled. Either it rained or it didn't, without warning us whether it would start full force or stop.

Heidricks, the most annoying man in the platoon, had a bar of soap in his shirt pocket. I was sure he was waiting for the rain opportunity. It was going to be a great story when he returned home, about how he took baths in the rain, one of those memories collected the way others posed for photographs. I had heard the stories before, about somebody who had used the rain for a shower. He did things for the sake of a future story back in Brooklyn. He dropped his gear and stripped to the waist, talking one other moron into doing the same. They lathered up in the rain, Heidricks declaring his cleverness. Soaped from head to waist, the rain stopped as immediately as it started. They stood dumbfounded, still holding the soap. All that remained was a mud puddle, two or three inches deep that they used to try to splash off the soap with muddy water. He won the platoon's dumb-ass of the day honors.

39

We set up an ambush site in a graveyard. It was the best location we had in a number of nights, out of noisy brush, briars and insects. We used graveyards before, and I liked them. The old graves had low, wide headstones with low concrete walls about eighteen inches high around the sides. They made good cover and solid protection. Inside, the grave's perimeter wall easily provided a two-man position, each position spaced ten meters apart.

The first platoon was assigned the kill zone along a narrow cart road, and we had rear security. The back side was a gently curving arc along the back row of graves, facing a flat area free of trees or brush. Rain had stayed away, and the dry night felt good, but I couldn't see ten feet in the blackness.

Sometime after we completed our set up, I began scanning the area with the starlight scope. I'd made mental images on the distances to the nearest trees and brush before dark, and it was time to compare them through the starlight.

I slowly panned the scope right to left. I stopped little more than half way across. No further than a hundred feet were three

VC sitting beside a large tree at the wood line. They sat talking quietly, rifles laying across their laps. I was beyond earshot, but they were relaxed as they sat side by side. It was the same as the night I spotted the big cat at the firebase, startled at the sight but quickly calmed.

I dropped the eyepiece out of the way to sight the direction over the top of the scope then looked again; they were at ten o'clock from my position. I told Keller, my RTO and handed him the scope to sight them while I aligned my rifle with the scope direction. I knew one of two things would happen: they would get up to move out, or someone else would meet them there. I believed they were waiting on others. We would sit, wait, and be ready.

Without a sense of urgency, I checked the position to my left, Viehl and Cerda, with the scope to see what they were doing. They were good, both sitting with backs to the headstone, unaware. Beyond them, our end position was anchored by Armstrong, one of the platoon veterans, and another man.

Keller watched while I got on the radio to call Delta 6, the CO. I called to notify him, and all other radio positions of the situation, hoping to avoid a repeat of two months earlier when the other platoon unnecessarily blew their claymore mines. This time everything was under control.

Slumped over the handset with my back against the headstone and hands cupped over the radio mouthpiece held to my chest, I called in a low, clear voice, "Delta 6, November 6 - Over." No response. I repeated several more times, "Delta 6, Delta 6, this is November 6. Over." Nothing. Dude, his former RTO had gone home; a new man was on the job.

"Shit, I can't believe this."

I stopped to take another look through the scope, handing the handset to Keller, whispering, "See if you can get Delta 6." Keller got nothing either.

I skipped Delta 6 and called for a commo check to rest of the company, "All Delta Kilos, all Delta Kilos, this is

November 6, if you hear me, break squelch twice." To break squelch, a radio operator pressed and released the talk switch on the handset without saying anything; it emitted a static sound. It was used as a means of nonverbal communication at night in order to eliminate extra noise. If they heard me, they would squeeze and release the switch twice. My earpiece crackled with low volume static of operators' response. I told Keller, "Everybody in the whole god damn company with a radio can hear me, but the dumb-asses in company headquarters." I quickly explained to everyone else. "Roger, this is November 6, I have three VC sitting in our kill zone. We're waiting, be ready." I got off the radio. I knew battalion headquarters monitored radio transmissions, and I hoped like hell they heard the silence by our own non-responsive command.

We were ready. Our rifles were sighted in and although out of our claymore's zone, we had our detonators at hand. Three or four minutes had passed since the sighting.

Then more VC walked up on the end position, between them and the claymores. Armstrong told me the next morning that he threw the first grenade.

40

Webster's dictionary defines a vicious circle as 'a situation in which the solution of one problem gives rise to another, but the solution of this, or of other problems rising of it, brings back the first, often with greater involvement'. It is a reasonable definition of war in general, and it is perfect for a really fucked-up situation.

I didn't know what was going on, but I knew grenade explosions, and I knew it didn't involve the three men I had been watching. Near pitch-black, I could barely see Keller sitting beside me. There was no good solution to a grenade battle. Grenades were answered with grenades. Dependence on luck to step forward was a big part.

It was too late to raise my head and shoulders above the grave stone to use the scope. The grenade tossing had started. It was impossible to know whose were inbound or whose were outbound, where they were thrown from, or where they were landing.

I threw my first to the front of the position to my left, then my second. I waited for the second explosion. Nothing. "Goddamn it - a fucking dud." Keller didn't carry frag grenades because of the weight and bulk the radio added to his rifle and ammo. I was listening, feeling for shrapnel flying in the dark, expecting to hear it hit the grave stones, maybe my helmet. I hoped most of the explosions were grenades thrown from my men. I wasn't counting, but we carried two per man; five of us on the three positions had ten grenades, including duds. Keller's and my claymores were useless; they were pointing to the front of our position.

Neither side fired rifles. The first to fire would have exposed their location by muzzle flash and tracer rounds. Without knowledge of their number, or where to expect return fire, it was common sense and survival instinct to not fire. I was aware too, that the other platoon had their unprotected backs toward us in case of a firefight from our side of the ambush. I didn't want them caught without cover.

I thought the VC must have appeared between my men and their claymores as the reason they weren't detonated.

I had forgotten about the original three VC, but knew they would have run away immediately. They were no longer a factor.

Six or eight grenades exploded in a period of a minute or less. It felt longer. The next morning, an equal number of duds were picked up, both ours and the wooden handled versions used by VC. From where some laid, between our position and the one to our left, I was thankful they were duds.

A cobra gunship was already on the way. We had recently been issued small strobe lights to carry on ambush. The size of a pack of cigarettes, they were new technology and their light visibility was five thousand feet. The company had three of them. Spaced out on our positions, they showed air support a triangulated position of friendlies on the ground. Smoke markers were useless at night.

The Cobra came across us on a low trajectory, firing pass with 2.75 inch rockets. The gun ship was invisible in the dark. I held my arm straight out, the strobe pointed toward its sound. Rockets struck well beyond the target area. I asked for the next run to be at least a hundred meters closer to us, but the second time was no better. I didn't know if he would risk firing any closer in the dark, or if Delta 6 even relayed my request. It didn't matter; the VC were long gone, and closer fire may have caused friendly-fire injuries.

The Cobra left. Illumination flares popped, lighting the area. Cerda and Veihl, positioned to my left were wounded and attended by medics. I watched the area to our front, shadows moving in the trees caused by flares coasting to the ground, swinging on their parachutes. Medevac was on the way. I didn't see the men before they were put on the chopper. I asked about them; both were alive was all I knew. I was sure that 93rd Evac would get them patched up.

After daylight, Medevac was called again. Two other men, Palmer and Morris, were barely able to stand. They were on the far right end of our line and not involved during the night. Neither man knew anything happened; they heard nothing and remembered nothing. They were sick with meningitis and were shipped off to the beaches at Vung Tao for recovery. I didn't see them for six weeks. Men in the field longed for such an illness, simply for the treatment, picking up seaweed from the beach every day. Vung Tao was an in-country R&R site.

After daylight, we walked the area for signs of possible VC wounds, but found nothing. I talked with Armstrong, who was on the end, trying to reconstruct exactly what happened. I wanted to know why or how they walked up on our positions, whether a random accident, or if they heard something that attracted their attention. He told me everything was quiet. Two or three VC walked up for no apparent reason. Maybe it was a mistake on their part, confused about the meeting spot at the large tree. They could have found the wires to the claymore mines. I couldn't understand why three of them were waiting under a tree, and the others walked to the graveyard.

I was pissed-off. My insides boiled from the night. It went from a plan that couldn't fail to a colossal screw-up. I'd rerun every minute so many times in my head. Delta 6's RTO didn't escape my ire when I saw him that morning; neither he nor the captain understood the concept of professionalism. If either of them had been alert, Keller and I wouldn't have wasted time on the radio. Maybe I would have panned the scope left far enough to catch the other VC moving. I blamed myself for not looking that far, not looking for the unexpected.

I was certain that I would see Cerda and Veihl in a few days, recuperating in the rear area; I never saw them again. Cerda was sent immediately to the hospital in Japan, which meant he was seriously hurt and eventually sent home.

The company First Sergeant came out to the NDP several days later with the message that Veihl died two days after the ambush. He asked me, "Do you want his home address, to send a letter to his family... or do you want me to do it?"

I thought a second, "No, you do it." I didn't know what I could say to his family. How could I make anything sound good or reasonable surrounding his death? I didn't know how to lie that much. The First Sergeant didn't know him, except by name; he could make up something.

I was numb to feelings of sympathy about Veihl. He and Cerda arrived the same day about two months earlier. He was quiet, and I didn't yet know much about him. A lean bean-pole in black-rimmed glasses, he looked like a kid, but I found out he was two weeks older than myself. I didn't feel like the age that he looked. He had curiosity about things going on around him; I liked that. He was becoming a good soldier, maybe had potential of being a squad leader, but bad luck intervened. Contrary to how I should have felt, I was angry more than anything; we had one man less in the platoon. That's what my life had been reduced to: numbness, dumb luck, and so little difference between life and death. Goddamn war. His name wasn't mentioned again in the platoon.

I wrote the letter to his family; it was forty-one years later. I talked with a younger brother on the phone, told him his brother was a good man, and I was sorry about his death. It wasn't a lie.

41

Beginning the night that Veihl and Cerda were wounded, five of the next eight nights were spent on ambush. A schedule could not have been designed to make anyone more fucking tired of rain, bugs and lack of sleep. Jesus, it got old going around the clock. Sleep was measured in minutes at a time on the rainy nights. Muscles were constantly drawn tight against the cold. The only hope for relief was with my nylon poncho liner, a double layer thickness of rip-stop nylon. It was light enough to be rolled tightly and carried in the side pocket on my pants. Wrapped around the neck and upper body, the cold rainwater sealed the fine weave, trapping some of my body heat beneath. One small move to break the seal was like having ice water dumped inside. The only real relief came the next morning on the first rest stop. I searched for ground in full sun instead of shade. The same sun I hated two months earlier in the dry season was coveted for the ten minutes it was possible to lie under. I shed my wet gear, and opened my still wet shirt to the waist. Blanketed by heat, I lay spread-eagle, eyes closed, slow, shallow breaths my only movement. Beads of sweat rose and ran, puddled in each hollow of my body from clavicle to navel, until it overflowed, dripping off like condensation, and I was still cold inside. The cold trapped beneath my skin went to the core of every bone.

#

Misery took a break. Good fortune came our way before the end of the eight days, when we were called into DiAn. I didn't question good luck. Once inside our barrack, I collapsed on my bunk for several hours of uninterrupted, merciful sleep Whatever plans they had cooked up next for us would be better than the shit we were doing; I welcomed any change.

The time off wasn't because higher command thought we needed rest. I doubt they gave a rat's ass. There was another reason. I didn't make note at the exact time because I didn't know our company commander disappeared. Usually a clerk or an alert RTO would catch wind of major events, but not that time. I thought the captain went to a briefing, but he never returned.

No official announcement was made, but a quiet good riddance celebration was held within the company. I believed and hoped that he was relieved because of his incompetence on either May 4, or just days earlier on ambush, when he couldn't be raised on the radio. Maybe somebody finally realized he was a leech on the infantry and on good men in our unit, or that he could and would get people killed. He should have been in an office, far away from the field. I never heard where he went, but hoped he wasn't assigned to another infantry company. Lieutenant Brav, the company XO, took over in the interim. Despite Shaw's departure, it was too late for me to regain enthusiasm for the war. The month of May had taken its mental toll. The only thing I looked forward to was a new CO; one I hoped would have some experience and common sense. In retrospect, it seems two points of time were important in war. The first period was to stay alive the first month in country and get familiar with daily life. The second was to live until the end of three months, when enough experience increased odds to stay alive. Of the men I knew, the majority were killed within the first three months. At the end of three months, I had seen all the war I wanted.

#

The next night the company was back to business with an air assault out for ambush. Lima had point. Before we stopped that night, I could only shake my head in amazement. It showed what a lack of experience could do. Their platoon leader and three other men died less than three weeks earlier. They lost the way to our coordinates, which meant the company was lost. We passed the site then backtracked too far. At 2200 hours we stopped. It was black, long past ability to see a map or recognize surrounding terrain, and damn sure too late to be walking around. We spent the night in the wrong place, but it was rainless, and that was fine with me. The plan for the next morning was to move to a site, set up a perimeter for the day and rest for the next night's ambush. We were headed to an eventual NDP destination so were also loaded with our ruck sacks and extra claymores for ambushes, adding bulk and weight to our regular gear.

We didn't rest that day. The second platoon, Mike, was on a patrol separate from the rest of the company and made contact with a small number of VC that morning. We were redirected to assist on the chase.

The rest of the company made it to a clearing waiting for orders when the battalion commander's helicopter landed. The second platoon was still thrashing around in the brush like a pack of hounds on the hunt. A wounded man was carried out. The colonel walked toward him, no doubt to offer words to the young man. I was certain I was going to overhear words of encouragement, how the soldier was doing a great job, his usual patronizing words that should fill him with the glory of war. Instead, the colonel received a first-class cursing as the soldier passed. I was shocked, although it was amusing. The colonel moved back closer to his helicopter.

We joined the fray, swept through thickets, unable to see more than a few feet in any direction. It was a typical day; a few bunkers and scattered remnants were found, but the VC disappeared like rabbits into the brush. Two men were wounded for their day's work.

As we were leaving, I got down on hands and knees and tossed a grenade back into a suspicious hole. As I got up to run, with the extra pounds on my back, I stumbled and fell about five feet from the hole. I had plenty time to think of how stupid that was, while my ears rang for awhile.

Our platoon took point to that night's ambush site, another day finished, another night ahead. We would rest the next day. The best I could do was to mark another X on my calendar.

42

I was glad to have Lieutenant Brav back as temporary company commander. He understood the essence of each day's mission, what was important, what wasn't; no bullshit. My mood improved, if not my enthusiasm. He was the exact opposite of Shaw, but I was sure he had no desire to be in the field again; he had already put in his time there.

After we moved out from our mis-oriented ambush site, we were picked up by Hueys at 0700, an unusual happening. I didn't know chopper pilots even got up that early. Any other time, I would have been suspicious of such timing and luxury, but I was tired of humping with the rucksacks. They flew us back to the Peanut Patch NDP, where we had been before. I thought it would be our new home, but no sooner had we been assigned our perimeter sectors and dropped our gear than we were radioed to load up again.

Chinooks arrived by 1000 hours, destination Phouc Vinh. The name was only vaguely familiar. None of the men in the platoon had ever been there. It meant nothing, but any place that had a real name, instead of a map coordinate destination, offered hope. We didn't have so much as a rumor for our mission, and such mental vacuums left much to imagination. I'd rather had some idea of expectations, and let the operations section save surprises for somebody else.

The big windowless tube of constant vibration and noise allowed no hint of the terrain below. I always enjoyed a preview of the ground that we might patrol. The ride was short, much shorter than flights to Lai Khe. The load ramp lowered and a twin prop C-130 taxied down a runway next to the chopper pad. I hadn't seen a runway or fixed wing aircraft anywhere I'd been and Phouc Vinh looked like a metropolis.

Minutes later, I sat alone in a wooden barrack's doorway with my gear lying on the ground beside me. There was still no word about a mission. The men milled around, talking. We faced an identical row of barracks across the narrow, hard-packed, dirt street. A company of grunts wearing Big Red One patches was packed up, ready to move out; maybe we were their replacements, I thought. Some of my men scouted around the area, asking questions, trying to gather information, rumors, local superstition, anything that would give us a focus. One absolute we knew; there was no need to put our gear inside the barracks – we wouldn't be using them.

A small convoy of two-and-a-half-ton trucks pulled up across the street, and men began the climb up the dropped tailgates. It was difficult. Loaded down with the weight and bulk on their backs, soldiers were pushed up and pulled onto the trucks. Watching them was like staring into a mirror. I didn't know who they were, but we looked the same, and I had to wonder if there were any differences. I knew they were headed toward misery somewhere from the look on their faces. Where didn't matter. They would be digging in a new NDP or humping patrol before the day was over. I knew our fate would mirror theirs in some way.

Each platoon carried an M-72 LAW (Light Antitank Weapon). It was a 66mm diameter rocket inside a plastic tube, designed to penetrate armored vehicles. It was a single use weapon, meant to fire then dispose.

One of the men climbing onto the back of a truck almost directly across the street had one strapped across his back. I was watching him load. Men grabbed his arms to pull, some pushed from below to help. The M-72 exploded inside the tube. Some of my men ran over, but there was nothing to be done. There was one more dead soldier; a grunt killed while climbing on the back of a truck. His expiration date found him. There were more to take his place. I sat, immune to feelings, or the value of life. The best I could do was wonder how much time he had left on his tour, think about how many patrols and ambushes he didn't have to go on. I wondered if he had rather died in a firefight and what his family would be told. He wouldn't be digging in or humping patrol that afternoon. The glory of war, it was what the military would call a weapon malfunction. No shit. The next day all M-72's were turned in; we no longer carried them, but most people didn't know why.

An hour later we reloaded the Chinooks and said good-bye to Phouc Vinh. Whatever our mission was there, it was done. I thought we may have gone to see a man die.

We flew to DiAn, our home base. We had reason to believe we were staying and shed our gear once more, sat and waited. Somebody didn't know what in the hell to do with us, but I didn't care, it still counted as a day. It would still earn an X on my calendar. After three hours, I received a quick briefing. Hueys were coming, and we were going to Highway 1, a few kilometers north of Saigon. It was back toward paddy country. The day's operation began with a 0700 chopper ride; ten hours and four rides later, we found a new home.

Our Hueys landed on dry rice paddies, hardly more than a hundred meters from Highway 1. I thought, 'How stupid is this? This is fucked-up, this close to a major highway. Shit, every VC and his brother can ride along and zero us in. The whole area will know where we are and can see the direction every time we leave.' I didn't want to be so close to a high-traffic highway, nor could I see the tactical thinking. We could have moved hundreds of meters further away from the highway and been out of sight.

It was 1700. Bunkers had to be dug before sleep. The first shovelful dug showed water in the bottom of the hole; the water level was less than a foot under the dry surface. Bunkers had to be dug four-and-a-half-feet deep and a bit wider. It was another long night. Men stood in holes of water, digging. The most frequent question was, "Who's the fucking genius that came up with this place?" The place got worse.

43

Any attempt to construct defensive positions in that rice patty was a farce. Men were standing in holes of water trying to shovel deeper. It was impossible to dig further than waist-deep in the water. Sandbags were filled with mud and stacked around the shallow, water-filled holes which were fine for dwarfs but otherwise useless. I hated getting into new sites late in the day. When we started in the evening, digging and sandbagging went into early morning hours.

I was assigned the sector facing the highway, adding insult, in my opinion. It was not enough to be so near, I had to be on the side of the perimeter to sit and watch traffic.

The colonel's chopper appeared late the next morning. That was a first for him. I thought maybe he was dropping by to check on Lieutenant Brav since Shaw was gone. I was busy when he landed and paid little notice, but did see there was someone else with him.

"Maybe it's somebody from S-3. They probably came out to get a close look at this shit-hole they stuck us in, so the dumb-asses can understand a map doesn't have to show a water symbol in a place to actually have water."

The colonel walked around and inspected the bunker layouts the way drill sergeants in basic training inspected bunks and shined boots. Surprised, I would've thought a battalion commander had better things to do, and I didn't think of it then, but it was likely a pretense to see how bad the place was. He didn't acknowledge the fact that we had dug a bunch of holes full of water. He didn't bother to check for depth either.

Following the inspection, I was called to the company CP. The extra person wasn't from operations; he was my new company commander, Captain Nolen. The first thing I noticed was he wore a First Infantry Division patch on each shoulder of his fatigues. That told me he had already served a previous tour of duty with our division. Previous combat division patches were worn on the right sleeve, current division patches worn on the left. Except for the built-in leeriness developed the previous few months, I had an immediate sense of relief from his presence. Why hadn't I had somebody like him when I arrived, unlike the previous idiot? He seemed normal, a little old-looking for a captain, relaxed and low-keyed. That's the way his nature turned out to be, but I would test his calmness in the months to come.

#

My platoon's strength was down to fifteen men, half the number I had when I arrived, and I didn't like it in the least. It was a third the number of regulation strength and was bloated with too many chiefs and equipment for which we had no use on patrol. The fifteen men included myself, the platoon sergeant, squad leaders, and six radio operators. Of the four or five men left, two of them made up the M-60 machine gun crew, and one with the M-79 grenade launcher. One thing we didn't need was six radios. The whole platoon was within voice range on patrol so four radios were left behind, and squad leaders demoted to riflemen until we got enough men to make squads.

#

Rain struck each day for the next four days. The ground was saturated, and with each rain our living conditions worsened. On day one, we lived in soft mud, and by day four, water stood three inches deep inside our sleeping quarters. There was no place to keep rucksacks or field gear dry. We couldn't even sit at our bunker and remove wet boots and socks to dry out after coming in off patrol. At mealtime I walked to the nearest dike, the only dry place to sit and eat from open cans of C-rations balanced on my knees. The unreasonable conditions put every man well beyond the normal complaints to a mutinous frame of mind. Most nights were ambushes and cold rains; afterwards there was no place to come in and rest in reasonable comfort. It added to the cumulative tiredness of the platoon.

We came in from patrol one afternoon and found a load of wooden shipping pallets dropped off by the supply chopper. They were dragged over, fitted inside our sandbagged sleeping area and with our air mattresses, we slept a couple of inches above water.

The first platoon had it worse. They dug-in at the lowest corner of the paddy. They returned from patrol to find their pallets floated up and over the sandbag walls of the sleep area. The entire corner of the paddy was under water. For amusement, the men resorted to launching themselves, running full speed with their air mattresses across the water, yelling 'surf's up!' With laughter from everyone around, it drove home the absurdity of our situation.

We didn't last for the standard two-week stint. Somebody finally realized rice paddies and the monsoons didn't make for an operational base. The eighth day after arrival, we left, defeated by rain, rising water, and misery. The trip back to DiAn meant a shower and hours of dry sleep. Sleep was always the highest immediate priority after arriving in a base camp. It recharged my whole physical and sometimes emotional systems, by getting off the wet ground and out of the sun. To have a few uninterrupted hours was a true luxury.

44

Our next mission began at 2300 hours the following night. It was an operation to encircle the village of Tan Heip, site of the May 4 battle, and seal off all entry and exit points. At dawn a search for enemy or a weapons cache would be made. I was familiar with the theory, a cordon and search operation, having studied it at the Infantry School. It was a legitimate operation if dictated by reasonably good intelligence, but I didn't look forward to any night operation. I had yet to experience any successful night movements. My confidence in the purpose of the operation wasn't that high. It sounded too much like another of the battalion commander's resume-building exercises although he didn't physically take part.

I already knew from May 4 that the village was little more than a two-hour walk outside DiAn. That night we moved out an hour before midnight. We were only half of the operation. Two companies, moving from different start points were to link up at 0300 hours. Knowing how screwed up night movements could be, I was greatly relieved to not be the point platoon for our company. Trying to follow a compass heading on a circular arc in the dark and meeting another unit doing the same was an insane thought. I was satisfied to not get shot at by friendly fire, a bigger worry than VC.

I had gotten some sleep in the afternoon to help last through the night. I remembered the terrain of scrub brush mixed with tall grasses and trees from our patrol on May 4. It was familiar even in the black, and it made movement bearable. There was no water, vines, or holes that could be teeth-jarring if found by a blind step.

We stumbled around, guessing our location until 0500 hours. It was two hours past rendezvous time and we never found the other company. We had no way to even know our own position until daylight, an hour later, when visual landmarks could be found. At dawn I walked up the line and found Captain Nolen to find out what our situation was. I got a shoulder shrug and a smile; he was as lost as everyone else. We held our position, in case anyone came our way, which they didn't. I never saw the village. We were the blocking force while the other company made the sweep, but did hear the search came up empty. I wasn't surprised by any part of the night.

By order of the colonel, every available man went on the seal. We didn't have any literal walking wounded, but we had men in the rear preparing to go on R&R, and some short-timers getting ready to ship out for home. It was common practice that those men would have a few days to launder uniforms, have proper rank and patches sewn on, get fresh haircuts, and simply decompress from the field before leaving. That night they would all have one more mission before departing. Combined, there were a dozen men in this group. Using a patrol spacing of one to two meters in the dark, they extended the linear coverage by some twenty meters total.

At 0800 we started our patrol back into DiAn. A three-quarter ton truck was sent out to pick up the extra men who were commandeered to go on the seal. They would resume their time off, preparing to leave. One of the men packed in the back of the small truck was Sergeant Rayborn, one of my squad leaders, who was going on R&R.

We were walking across the flat, open scrub-covered plain when I heard the explosion. I couldn't see the truck coming down one of the old cart roads across the open area behind me, but it didn't take long to know what it was.

Sergeant Rayborn went to 93rd Evac Hospital instead of R&R. He was lucky. Sergeants Ike Hall and Hamp Carter from one of our platoons were both preparing to go home in a few days. Neither lived. They were sitting in the wrong place on the back of the truck. There were more casualties from the other company.

I wondered if the battalion commander had any regrets for unnecessarily ordering men to participate; men who had no business going on the operation. I doubted he included that part of the story when he recounted his village seal operation; it was all just part of the job.

Normally the front floors and sometimes the rear bed floors of trucks were reinforced by a layer of filled sandbags, in case of explosions. I didn't know if that was the case on their truck. The immediate word was that the truck hit a mine. That may well have been the case, but I suspected it ran over an unexploded mortar or artillery round. It was in a remote area unused by any kind of vehicles – a random case of bad luck. In a case of closing the gate after the horses are out, a metal detector was brought out and the remainder of the road was swept for mines. Nothing was found.

45

We moved around in gypsy fashion, digging in for short stays around the area north of DiAn until we moved back into the Peanut Patch NDP. It was good to have bunkers already dug. It was the only perimeter where I'd been that had insect life, inhabited by annoying flies and black beetles. It was a good base for patrols, well above the flat paddy land to the south. Several villages were scattered within a few kilometers' radius, and where there were villages there were VC.

Rains always seemed to hold off until the most inopportune times. Some days were dry until we had a five-minute downpour just as we had moved into ambush positions, insuring a wet night. Sometimes it fell in sheets while we squeezed into our covered sleeping area behind our bunkers. Our poncho roofs invariably failed from a poorly lapped seam or drooping edge. Leaking drips turned nights into Chinese water torture, or objects floated around us from rain running down the insides of sandbags. Our communal discomfort was often elevated to a level that all we could do was surrender to the irrational laughs of lunatics sharing defenseless misery.

#

Half-way to our ambush site one afternoon, we were stopped and air lifted to provide a blocking force for an ARVN unit's sweep operation. It ended at 1800 hours without results, and we were redirected with new sets of coordinates to set up two ambushes for the night. The company was divided by platoons into ambush sites about six hundred meters apart. Both locations were set on the same well-defined cart path that connected crops and villages.

Two platoons plus company headquarters stopped at the first site. We filed past to move to our location.

"Don't forget where we are, just down the road - don't get excited and shoot our asses tonight if something happens," I told the platoon leader who was going to set up on their kill zone. I had a joking smile, but it was only a half-joke. "Remember, bullets travel a hell of a lot further than six-hundred meters, and we're going to be to your left front." I pointed out our approximate destination to their lieutenant, as a reminder that we were not out of range, nor out of the line of fire if somebody got crazy.

"We've gotcha covered - I promise not to shoot you tonight," he laughed.

We crossed the road and into medium thick, waist-high scrub before we turned left and walked parallel with the road. We moved through the brush for four or five hundred meters and stopped for our staging area. One of the men spoke up.

"Hey Lieutenant, there's somebody down by the trees on our right rear - about two hundred meters away."

From the distance they looked like young men, huddled together under a small clump of trees. No weapons were showing, but they looked suspicious. They were watching us, but it was still forty-five minutes before curfew, and they could make it to the village a few hundred meters beyond them before dark. If it got dark on them, they were considered VC. I didn't like them watching our movements, and suspected they might go to the village and report us for whatever reason.

With so much daylight remaining, we stopped at least a hundred meters out from our ambush site. The platoon sat down in the chest-high bush, out of sight. Later, two squad leaders and I walked onto the site to scout it out.

"Shit, this is no good. This whole goddamn place is flat. There's not one spot of cover. Shit, fucking S-3 sees a fucking road on a map that makes a turn and figures it will make a good site without knowing shit what it looks like."

I radioed our site situation to the CO then looked around the area for a better location. There wasn't one. The entire area was flat with zero cover.

"What are we gonna do, Lieutenant?" One of the sergeants asked.

"This is where we'll be, but if we have trouble, we'll be up shit creek. This fucking place is bad. Listen, put the best men on the road for the kill zone; I'll take the newer guys on the rear security."

I briefed the rest of the platoon, and we sat low and quiet until the sky darkened. We got up and slipped away in the fast fading light. A fresh crop, grown only enough to color the ground green was planted in the bend in the road. It was a terrible place to be. We lay on the crop, each man forming a clear lump on the flat surface; I was at the rear, facing the scrub brush we had come through. Still low on manpower, we were spread thin.

Less than an hour after we settled in, automatic weapons fire started in full force. I thought the other platoons had blown their ambush and grabbed the radio handset to listen. No claymores were blown, and the radio was silent. I thought, 'What the fuck is going on? Nobody talking?' After a minute, I radioed one of the other platoons. They were thinking the same about us.

I raised up enough to see over the bush. All of the firepower we were hearing was coming from the clump of trees where we saw the group before dark. They were firing into the bush where we had stopped and waited for dark. That was why we didn't move into position until the last minutes. I had a mental smirk knowing we had tricked the bastards; I knew then they were watching to get a fix on our night position, but we moved. AK-47's were popping, and tracers lighting up nothing but empty space. The tracers were the normal red except one weapon had green ones. It was the first time I had seen green tracers. I was curious about them and the difference from standard tracers.

We didn't return fire. It would have been stupid at minimum to return fire without any type of cover. When the VC got no reaction from their attack they began yelling and got wilder in their firing, spraying all around. I was amused until I heard a thud hit the soft, damp ground on my left side. I thought, 'There's one guy in that bunch that knows what the hell he's doing, spraying the whole area low.' I aligned myself like a weathervane, steel helmet pointing directly toward the firing while I grabbed two handfuls of vegetation and pulled myself tight against the ground.

Artillery and gun ships were called in by the CO to do their work, but the VC had dispersed. In two hours, it was quiet again with the exception of occasional rounds popped off by the returned and still defiant VC.

By 2300 hours, partial moon had risen. Clouds and rain stayed away, but visibility was something we did not want that particular night. I looked down the rear security line and saw one man sitting up on the far end, eating C-rations. Occasional rounds were still popping off by the VC. I could see the moonlight reflect off the shiny underside of the lid on his can like a weak flashlight. There was enough light I could see it was one of the newbies, and he was destined for an early morning ass-chewing for being a fucking idiot and endangering the whole platoon with his late-night snack.

Gearing up at day break, Sergeant Dennis and Specialist Reps came up and told me three VC came down the road at 0230, but with our poor position they thought better of blowing the ambush and giving our location. I had opened my mouth to say something quite to the contrary, but I didn't. I just nodded instead. Probably couriers, they were the reason for the early activity, to try to give warning or protection. That night, dumb luck was on their side. Sometimes common sense was the most important thing.

I hoped the next morning we would go down to the tree line and pick up the VC's trail. I would have bet anything it would lead to the village less than a kilometer in the distance and maybe a weapon cache would turn up. We didn't do that; there was no such thing as an impromptu mission. We already had an assignment for the day and nothing was going to change it, no matter how routine it was. I put another X on my calendar that night.

46

The morning after we avoided the VC's ambush, we moved back into DiAn for eight days. It was good to have a real roof over our heads for awhile. Four of the nights were ambushes, with another cancelled, and two days were company sweep operations. Those had a body count of two enemy KIA's and three POW's, but we were always on the rear when contact was made, so none of the action involved my platoon. For us, it was just another day.

At the end of eight days we dug in a new NDP, and I got six new men in one day to help replenish the platoon's strength. I was tired of digging NDP's, and receiving six men at once wasn't appreciated. It was like teaching a third of the platoon what to do. They were split up and assigned to experienced men to learn the do's and don'ts of the field. Our platoon had not had any direct contact in awhile, and I worried it may have given them a false sense of security. I suffered that myself if not careful. It was tiring, boring crap for me. I was already counting the number of days until R&R, hardly more than a month and a half away. It was the nearest thing I had to look forward to.

Our new NDP was uninspiring, located only three or four klicks outside DiAn, on the huge plain that stretched out on the north side. We were so close to our base camp I was curious why the hell they put us there. It was hard to believe there were any tactical reasons. The area could be covered easily by armor units, artillery, or mortars from DiAn without our need to be there, but I didn't get to ask questions about such operational decisions.

We were on the edge of a region covered by scrub brush hiding small mounds of ground about a foot high and maybe twice as wide. They looked like petrified, oversized ant mounds. They were unavoidable, to step or stumble over, while patrolling through the waist-high scrub.

Bunker locations were laid out on the perimeter before digging began. Using normal spacing for overlapping fields of fire coverage, my own bunker had one of the large mounds directly in front of the ground-level firing port, partially blocking the field of fire. I knew it was wrong in theory, we dug it anyway.

The colonel must not have had anything to do that day and dropped by in his chopper. He walked around the perimeter inspecting our layouts and spotted the blocked view of the firing port. That was followed with the 'I'm disappointed in you, Lieutenant' speech for such a tactical infraction, and we had to dig a new bunker five feet to one side. He was the same pain in the ass on the ground as he was flying around. I knew the hump was there. We laid it out that way because it didn't matter, and if he knew the ground as well as he knew the view from his helicopter he would have known it too. We were never going to use the bunker except to store our rucksacks until the bottom covered with rainwater. The firing ports were six inches above ground level at the maximum, and it was impossible to see anything except the bottom of surrounding scrub brush with visibility measured in a matter of feet. As always, better firing positions were offered from the roof and the sandbagged sleeping area. Common sense never prevailed in the face of regulations however, or in a colonel who had never spent a night in a perimeter bunker.

Nothing was different in our operational diet of patrols and ambushes. Reports of VC close by always floated around, whether official intelligence or not. An ARVN ambush reported spotting a hundred and fifty, and other reports from one source or another of large numbers of VC in the area. I wondered why we didn't hear of more contact with VC instead of simply of sightings. I got to the point where I believed it was all a bunch of shit, more rumor than fact. On point one day we found a large number of recently occupied bunkers, but the camp was empty. It probably caused another report of large numbers of VC in the area. That was a highlight of that patrol, but mundane distractions more often ruled the day.

#

My point man stopped. He walked upon a gully, closer in size to a small ravine, running perpendicular to our path. It was the largest one I had seen, twelve-to-fifteen-feet wide and at least eight-feet deep with vertical walls. Gullies of various sizes were scattered across the countryside and would fill with flash floods following heavy rains. A powerful, rapid rush of water was why they were so deep for the width and sides so vertical; hours later, they would be empty again. Even though it was dry, we didn't have a rope to assist with a crossing, and it would take forever the get the company across.

I wasn't going to have the patrol slowed with that ordeal. I radioed the situation back to the captain; the company could take a break for awhile. I sent a small patrol in each direction to look for a crossing point. One patrol hadn't moved a hundred meters when they radioed, "We found a place to cross." An uprooted tree weakened by the washed-out gully had fallen straight across. I was hopeful at best until I saw the massive tree. I'd never noticed trees that big before, easily eighteen inches in diameter at the small part. "Damn, this is our lucky day. What a break." It was as perfect and solid as any bridge. A blind man could have walked it. I reported our good luck to the CO., and my platoon continued across effortlessly.

On the next break, Captain Nolen caught up with me. He wasn't smiling. "Don't ever cross anything like that again."

I thought, 'What the fuck is he talking about? Hell, it didn't need handrails,' but I could sense that he was mad as hell about it. I took it that either he didn't have good balance or didn't like heights, and made a mental note for no balance contest on patrol.

#

On our last day in the NDP, we packed up everything and headed out for an ambush outside the village of Tan Heip. It was where I was wounded six weeks earlier and I was excited about the prospect of returning to satisfy my curiosity about the area. It was another split-company operation; two ambushes were out with two platoons in each one. It was a quiet night and before we began the hump back to DiAn the next morning the captain gave the company time to look around the area. It was the first time any of us had been back to the specific area.

I entered from the direction opposite the familiar one and wandered off alone to see the area I didn't know before. The first place I found was what Reps had described as 'a low place' after he made his way back to the platoon on May 4. The low place turned out to be a small gully, five to six feet deep that wound its way alongside the village from below where our platoon's position was. I slid down in the gully near the village and walked back toward where I had been.

I thought, 'Why the hell didn't he say it was a fucking gully? Jesus Christ, he was from Colorado and should know what the fuck a gully is.' I wished I had known that day what it looked like. It was too late to change events. Of course, if the VC had caught us moving along a gully and dropped some grenades in on us, it would have been shit city.

Shallow water still covered the bottom from the last rain. A water snake swam across in front of me but I couldn't recognize it as poisonous and let it go its way. "Besides I'm not going to be back here. Maybe you'll bite a VC some day." Further along lay a skull and a few miscellaneous bones, the largest a femur. The skull was missing the lower jaw. "Where the hell could all the other bones have gone?" Looking over the top edge, I was standing at the wooded edge of the clearing, damn close to the spot where the VC fired the RPG at me. It was ironic, wondering if the skull might have belonged to the same man. "That would be poetic justice." The femur still had a light bit of tissue attached, unlike the skull. I shook what I took as sand from the skull and said, "You're going back to DiAn." Mounted scepter-like on a long stick, the MP's on the gate only shook their heads as we filed through. I sat it on a shelf beside my bunk, and it was still there the next time or two we came back in, but was stolen or otherwise removed while I was out in the field; disposition unknown. That afternoon we packed up for a return to Thunder Road.

47

My platoon was the first to take in the new landscape as we walked up the dirt entrance to Thunder II. The firebase was our new home for the next two weeks.

"I don't know what's in those drums, but I'll bet they'd make a hell of an explosion. You think they're expecting something we don't know about?" I was talking about the first things I noticed. Several fifty-five gallon drums were laid on their sides, half buried in the gentle slope outside the concertina wire perimeter. Detonation cord made a number of wraps around each one. It made no difference to me whether they contained napalm or diesel fuel, they were deadly looking, and added to my sense of security.

I had high hopes when they told us we were going back to a fire base on Thunder Road. I expected a rerun of my experience at Caisson 6. My next observation was that artillery firebases were not equal on Highway 13. Our previous duty at Caisson 6 was as close to heaven as we were going to get while wearing field gear. Thunder II was at the other end of the spectrum. Cooling trees of the rubber plantation were mere memories; there were no trees of any kind nearby. The base had a feeling of remoteness hanging over it, like there was nothing around for miles. It looked well-worn and scruffy, uninviting. I never knew exactly where we were in relation to Lai Khe or any other known landmark. All I knew was that we were on Highway 13.

A short distance out front of the perimeter, the red clay road ran straight for kilometers. No trees grew close to it on either side. My platoon's sector on the perimeter had two advantages. We were the front, facing the road and furthest distance from artillery noise, and the company mess tent was set up right behind my bunker. We could hear the cooks talking and were always the first to know when chow was ready. That made us first to the chow line.

Our first briefing took place at the CP as soon as we dropped our gear. The roll of the dice put my platoon out on three ambushes that night. That had a bad sound to it immediately. The distances were two, four, and six klicks down the road from the firebase. I thought, 'Oh shit. There's going to be some scared bastards out there tonight.' Platoon strength was back up to twenty-five men including myself. That made two ambushes with eight men each, and one with nine. At least one third of the men were still new. Another third didn't have the kind of experience needed to operate on their own, at least to do it and not be scared shitless. There was already a degree of apprehension upon arrival at a new location until we had a look around, getting a feel for it. To send a few handfuls of men out that far in the boonies on ambush, on the first night, could be considered cruelty. Every ambush during our two-week rotation was squad-size, with only one squad per night. The rest of the platoon patrolled or swept for mines the next morning. In those two weeks, we never saw any sign of use or of VC passing through the area.

Small ambushes often had a nervous twitch by the nature of their size. An eight- or nine-man squad was spread so thin it was difficult to set up a decent size kill zone as well as provide rear security, using two men per position to alternate watch. Imaginations struck an elevated level for squads out at night. Strange noises would be heard, and if someone stared at anything for more than a few seconds, it would start moving. At night, the eyes had to constantly scan and not fix on one spot. It wasn't too unusual to get a radio report about hearing unspecified sounds. They could usually be calmed down by a few minutes of talk on the radio, when rational thoughts returned.

The other type of report was of visual contact. That happened one night. I knew the squad leader well enough to know he shouldn't have been a squad leader. The fact that they were as far out as we sent an ambush didn't bode well. I wasn't surprised when the whispered situation report came over the radio. There was no return to normal for the squad, positive they spotted too many VC to engage. The captain decided to send some armor to bring the squad back.

"I bet this is a bunch of horseshit. I'm going down with the armor," I told my RTO. "You stay here; no need for you to go. I'm going to see what the fuck is happening. If Captain Nolen asks, tell him where I am." Whatever their story, as if I didn't know, I wanted to hear it first. An APC was fired up, sitting at the wire. I told the driver, "I'll be on top."

It was 2300 hours. Two M-48 tanks and the APC hustled down the road at high speed, an interestingly eerie ride in darkness. If I was eating dust I didn't know. All I could make out were the hulking forms of the tanks. The only sounds were from engines and tracks slapping the hard-packed road by the fast moving armor. It took a few minutes to reach the squad's location. The armor stopped then each vehicle made a ninety-degree pivot left to face the wood line. The tanks switched on their big Xenon searchlights, and the wood line lit up from the millions of candlepower. Blinding was the word. The squad stayed in cover by the trees until the armor arrived, then ran out to the road. I was relieved they had our starlight scope with them and didn't leave it.

For the next few minutes, both tanks bombarded the trees for maximum coverage, sprayed with .50 caliber and 7.62mm machine guns. I took advantage of the situation to use up my old ammo, and fired my seventeen magazines as fast as I could. My rifle barrel changed color, one hot piece of metal, but I may as well have been using a pea shooter; I could barely hear it over the firepower blasting away. When they ceased fire, I thought that was it, time to head back. I was wrong. Cobra gunships arrived and did their part, making sequential-firing rocket runs for more destruction of the trees. All in all, it was a display of firepower of which I would never want to be on the receiving end. I was sure it was time to call it a night, but nope, not yet. Artillery rounds began exploding above, illumination flares burning their own version of light. The terrain lit up with constantly changing light as they floated down beneath their parachutes. Shadows danced and darted around from the multiple sources of drifting luminance under the black sky. I borrowed a few full magazines from one of my men, and we swept on-line from the road into the wood line, close to a hundred meters away.

Was I surprised that nothing was found? Hell no. The only spooky part of the night was the canisters falling after the flares ignited. The empty cylinders flipped end-over-end in the free fall and sounded like a jug band warming up - whouhm, whouhm, whouhm all the way to the ground. I kept looking up behind me, thinking one on them was going to land on me at any second. I wondered how heavy they were, how fast they were falling, and if it would kill me if I got hit. I didn't want anything to screw up my R&R coming up. I gave my steel pot a whack on the top to make sure it was on my head good. We headed back at 0100 hours, packed up and left for DiAn on the last day of June. I was glad to leave after two weeks, and felt a little sorry for the artillery and armor crews stuck there for the duration.

In appreciation of the close proximity of the mess tent, I got up at 0530 that morning and gave the cooks a hand. It wasn't unusual. When it rained at night, I would scramble from our leaky, low-roofed quarters and go there. It was empty from evening chow until breakfast. The cooks used sawhorses topped by wide boards for cooking and serving, and I found I could sleep on the boards comfortably. That morning when they were set up, I took my place on the cook's line and fried eggs to order as the men came through.

48

The company relaxed in DiAn for a night and part of the next day. The men had a chance to drink beer, catch a movie, and make their rounds at the PX to restock on personal supplies. Mid-afternoon, we humped out to a NDP where we had been before, near the village of Tan Heip.

November platoon took point going in then had ambush that night. The battalion commander had taken to sending his observation helicopter out to pick up platoon leaders so we could get an aerial view of our upcoming ambush site. I was excited about it at first, but it often took time that I needed for other things. Also, the view from above had little value compared to a ground-level look. That was why the battalion CO was such a pain in the ass directing us when he was flying around watching. He never had a clue what it was like walking down there. Since it was our first night out since moving down from Thunder Road, the rain took the opportunity to make sure we were wet for the night.

We met up with the company the next morning at a resupply point where we spent most of the day before moving to that night's company-size ambush. We were near our site when we ran into Alpha Company – more like we bumped into them by accident. I stood close enough to overhear the conversation between the two company commanders and compare map readings. Captain Nolen was telling Alpha's CO, "Here's where we are ... we have ambush right here tonight," pointing to his map.

The other company moved out, and I passed word through the platoon about what was going on. "They are lost, bigger than hell." It was a bad thought that they would have a compass man up front who couldn't follow a course then have a platoon leader behind him who was dumb enough to follow. I could understand a squad maybe off course, but the thought of a whole company made me glad I wasn't in that unit. All we could say was "Hey, good luck guys."

Our company stopped a good distance from our site to wait for near dark. Captain Nolen sent me to scout out the location. On the map it was showing a well-defined, natural triangular shaped terrain fronting a cart road. I took a squad for a visual and reported it looked just as the map showed. The captain asked, "Is there enough space to get the company in?"

"Yes sir, it looked big enough to me," although it wasn't like I'd measured it. I never stopped and studied spots where I was going to be. It was more of a casual look as we walked slowly beyond the site, turned around and walked back, in case anybody was watching. That was the second time I found out what the captain didn't like. He about exploded in his own quiet way when he saw it. By his standards, it was too much a tight squeeze for the company. We couldn't expand the site. He chewed my ass out about how the whole company was jeopardized if we had heavy contact. I let it bounce off my back, thinking he was overly cautious; it was a perfectly fine place to me even it was a bit tighter than usual. I had been in worse.

An hour and a half later Alpha Company called. They had spotted about forty VC coming our way. Everyone got on full alert, but we never saw or heard a thing. It became another one of those reports of activity that vanished. 'Why the hell didn't they do something about it if they spotted them?' It was like a sighting of a Sasquatch that vanished into thin air.

Back at our NDP at 1030 hours the next morning, we had the day and night off. I went by supply our last time in DiAn and picked up my first pair of standard issue OD underwear. I wanted them to wear in the NDP. It was impossible to do in the hot, dry season; even with partial cloud cover I still got sunburned.

The next day we shared our NDP with another company and had a party-type meal, considering we were in the boonies. Surprise, it was July 4. Nobody realized it until we got up that morning.

49

Our new home most resembled a chicken barn. Although lacking physical evidence or smell of animal husbandry, I was reminded of a chicken brooding house. Long and narrow proportions, it was made entirely with corrugated roofing metal, and nobody planned for ventilation when it was built. I didn't know why they would put our entire company inside one building, but it was dry, and we didn't have to dig so it suited me.

We were alongside Highway 13 outside the northern edge of Saigon. The highway was a paved two-lane there, but as it went north it became a considerably narrower dirt road. We had returned to the general area where we dug in a perimeter a month earlier, only to find ground water a foot below the surface. The whole region was low and flat. There would be no digging that far south until the dry season returned.

Days until R&R were ticking away. When not on missions, my attendance was more body than mind; I could smell the coming of temporary freedom, and daydreaming was almost a full-time job. R&R meant I would have been in-country about six months. No one went on R&R before their half-way mark, so they wouldn't have to return to more time remaining in country than they had used.

Even better, Sherry and I would celebrate our second wedding anniversary in Hawaii, and after I returned, the end of my tour in the field would be near. We rotated out after six months because the life expectancy of company-grade officers was poor. I wasn't particularly thinking about leaving the field, only that I knew it would happen. It was one of the very few major changes that I had patience in waiting for since I had no certain date.

Another reason for the wait for R&R was my birthday; I thought I might need to be twenty-one to have a drink in a restaurant. The idea of an ID check and 'sorry we can't serve you' would have sent me over the edge.

Monsoonal rain pounding on the overhead metal was a pleasurable sound, knowing how it would be if we were under the usual dripping, leaky poncho roof. My platoon was in the very back of the building, offering more privacy and not bothered by other platoons walking through our area.

#

It was nice to see a change in terrain. It was an improvement. Most of our area covered open, flat ground, but across Highway 13 it became unusually good. Shade and easily traversed ground was welcome. We walked under or through tall coconut palms, banana trees, and a host of unrecognizable vegetation. Walking along one day, Sergeant Dennis reached up and plucked a small cluster of large marble-sized, green-skinned something. I had no idea what it was.

"Squeeze the end and pop the inside into your mouth," he told me. His eyes and memory never failed. He had seen them before.

"This isn't some kind of green crap, is it? Is it ripe?" I was thinking of unripened persimmons.

"It's good; you'll like it." He popped one in his mouth.

I squeezed the soft, thick outside rind. Something slippery and soothing hit my tongue, the size of a peeled grape but much easier to slide around inside my mouth, "What is this?"

"I don't know, but if your mouth is dry, this will take care of it."

"Yeah, no shit. It has a hard center. Are you supposed to eat it?" I was wondering why the things didn't grow everywhere.

"Nah, just let it slide around in your mouth, then spit it out."

I would've filled my pockets with them, but we were on the move, and I never saw any others. It must have been a fruit, growing in grape-like clusters, but I didn't know if it was wild or cultivated by the villagers. I thought back to all those afternoons, months earlier in the dry season, when I was out of water and couldn't even spit, as the sweet and slimy seeds slid around in my mouth, filling it with a kind of heavenly moisture.

#

Concertina wire secured our perimeter, along with the usual observation posts, but most of the security was needed at the entrance from the highway. The locals were quick to start their afternoon offerings, edging in as close as they could.

I regularly bought French bread to enhance the C-rations. The idea was to slice the loaf part-way through lengthwise, heat the rations if possible, and pour along inside the bread - a C-ration sandwich. I was the king of ham and lima beans, the most dreaded of all meals, and it seemed like they were one meal every day for me. The bread was tasty, but full of tiny, black bugs that were flicked out where it was sliced. They were throughout the loaves but at least unnecessary to see while eating. The fresh bread was worth overlooking slight imperfections. The bugs had been baked too so were presumed harmless.

The crowd grew the longer we were there. One day Captain Nolen decided he wanted them away from pushing in at our wire gate. Attempts to communicate the need for them to stay further from our perimeter failed, and somebody tossed a gas grenade in front of our compound to back them away. A consideration missed was wind direction, and we were downwind. It sent the whole company scrambling for gas masks or running for fresh air. The company-wide question was, "Who was the dumb ass who threw the grenade?"

The crowd dispersal episode surprised me, but confirmed the cautious nature of our normally easy-going CO. I believed he was overly cautious at times. We had point one day coming in across the open flat that stretched northeast of our NDP. Walking through short grass, the front men closed up their five-meter spacing formation prematurely, yakking, maybe carrying out a little horseplay. They were within two-hundred meters of our perimeter, and it was the only thing remotely close to us. The captain radioed up to spread our formation back out, and as soon as we got in I received a first class ass-chewing, the other platoon leaders got a warning, then he chewed the whole platoon's asses. Afterward, we stayed in standard formation all the way to the wire. I probably should have been more appreciative of his determination for our safety.

#

The day came when Captain Nolen needed a new radio operator. I thought I could help him out on that and offered mine. Keller had several months of RTO duty, was good at the job, and was as worthy of the position promotion to company headquarters as anyone. I figured the son of a Texas preacher would be a better fit with the captain, who brought his own Bible to the field and read it daily. Both men were the quiet, soft-spoken type, and I was sure Keller would welcome the chance be out of my not so quiet or soft verbal range.

#

Enemy contact had severely diminished over the past month or so. I thought it may be in part due to the monsoons, misery at night shared by both sides. After the Tet offensive, many enemy units were caught withdrawing from the Saigon area, or trying to move back in after reinforcement, to prepare for another offensive push. Either direction, they suffered heavy casualties when intercepted.

Our only contact from operations in the new area was a small fire fight on patrol one day. We were the rear platoon, as usual, when rounds began popping up front. Radios were fairly quiet, meaning their lead squad probably handled the contact, so I found a good tree to sit behind and waited. Five minutes later, the front platoon had captured two VC, one male, one female, with no casualties on either side.

By the time I made it to the front of the formation, both were standing motionless, blindfolded, hands tied behind. Sergeant Dennis struck quick with the butt of his M-16 to the torso of the man. I jumped forward, but I was too late to stop him. Captain Nolen shot me a glance of disapproval, to get Dennis under control. It was already done. Dennis was one of those who truly hated the VC to the point that he snapped. The company turned around and went home, the point platoon took the male, and we took the female, separating them from any communication. They were picked up by a chopper and moved to brigade headquarters for interrogation and possibly the chance to change allegiances. There was a unit named Kit Carson scouts made up of former Viet Cong, and in theory they could offer information on specific area tactics, logistics, or other intelligence.

#

The colonel sent his chopper out one afternoon for me to do an air recon of our ambush site that night. It was a week before I was to leave for R&R, and a day when I didn't feel good. I wasn't totally sick but queasy enough not to want to screw around doing anything nonessential, like an air recon. I climbed in with my M-16 and one magazine of ammo, unaware I was going up with a cowboy, as pilots wanted to be if given the chance.

"You know where we're going?" was the only thing I said to him.

"Yep, I've got it on the map here."

It wasn't that far from our NDP, and there was nothing special that required foreknowledge on my part. I was content to do a slow fly over and go back home. As always the aerial perspective didn't mean much since we weren't going to be lying in the tops of trees, looking down. Besides, there wasn't much to see through the light canopy, except by the pilot.

"I think I saw someone down there," he said.

I didn't see anything and thought, 'so what? Let's get the hell out of here,' but he took it as his personal responsibility to fully search the area by cutting tight donuts in the air with the fucking helicopter just above treetop level. He must have been new in country. I wasn't looking for anybody on the ground. We had one rifle and eighteen rounds of ammo on board unless he had something hidden. In my mind, I'd much rather be shot at on the ground than sitting in something that a reasonable breeze would blow around like a dragonfly. I was glad to get back and report.

"Yes sir, I got a good look at it. It looks okay," I told the captain.

There wasn't much to the site, no paths or roads where we might expect travel. A small tributary ran along beside us, and it was too small for boat movement of any kind. The ground was familiar. It was the damp, hard-packed black mud that flourished in deep shade and moisture that I hadn't seen since we patrolled along the Dong Nai riverbanks months earlier. I wasn't about to lie on the mud all night and found enough banana tree leaves and downed palm fronds to cover the ground.

It was an uneventful night, but I could hardly see things when I got up in the morning. When the men looked at me, they squinted, not getting too close.

"Your eyes are all swollen," one of them said.

"Swollen? How in hell could my eyes get swollen lying here?" Of course I couldn't see them, only the feeling of looking through small slits, but I could feel them with my hands.

"I saw some rats running around last night. Maybe it was one of them," was one contribution.

"I'm pretty damn sure I would have known if rats had been on my face."

"Well, it's more than swollen; you have big purple splotches all over your face."

"Jesus... what the fuck?" I looked all over and around the leaves I slept on - maybe it was some kind of sap, or bugs, but saw nothing. It didn't take long to think, 'I am a week from R&R; I don't need this shit happening.' Nobody else had it, and nobody was getting close to me.

A glance in the mirror was scary - purple, amoeba-shaped blobs covered my face and neck. It was tender to the touch. I was about to go into a medical panic, thinking how long it could stay, and I didn't want to go on R&R looking like a freak. 'Hell, they may not let me out of the country.'

The doctor from battalion headquarters arrived by chopper within a few hours. My only question was "Do you know what it is?"

"No, I haven't seen it before, but I'll bring some ointment back for you to use on it," he assured me.

The son of a bitch never came back, not a word, no cream, ointment, nothing, and there was no going on sick-call for me.

I was still able to walk and function, in perfect condition by infantry standards.

By the next morning it had spread onto the tops of my shoulders. I put on my field gear to move out, but the tenderness under the straps was enough discomfort that I made my own medical call. "Fuck it, I'm not going to haul this stuff around all day. I'm not going on patrol today," giving the platoon sergeant the platoon for the day. I neither notified nor got permission from the captain to hang back.

"Where is your gear," he asked, the company ready to move out. He had an unhappy look on his face.

"I'm not going out today, sir. This has spread to my shoulders and it's so sore I can't wear those straps all day." His face got even unhappier, like I was gold-bricking, but I didn't care how pissed-off he was. They could do without me for one day. The centers of the splotches on my face had lightened from purple to merely red, the swelling was down, but the irregular shaped edges were well defined. It was less than a week until R&R and it wasn't disappearing with any great speed. 'That sorry-ass doctor.'

When going on R&R, it was usual to leave the field three days prior in order to get uniforms laundered, proper patches sewn, haircuts and personal needs taken care of. There was no duty or interference by the company.

The day before catching the chopper to the rear was my birthday, my twenty-first. Nobody knew it, and I neither mentioned nor celebrated. It was just another patrol day. I didn't want to bring any attention to my age since I was self-conscious about it within the platoon. There were a number of men in their twenties, and I wanted to keep our relationships strictly on a rank basis. Besides, we never celebrated or knew anyone's birthday the entire time I was in the field. I guess there was no reason to bring it up.

I got up the next morning all smiles, packed my gear, and told the platoon to have fun on patrols and ambushes until I got back. I was Hawaii-bound. My face, neck, and shoulders were not completely free of red outlines, but they decreased a little each day, and I thought maybe a light suntan would hide anything left; I was happy to look human again. I looked at the Xs on my calendar. Jesus and I were moving along.

50

I had waited six months, six long months, for that flight to Honolulu. "I'll see you in six months" were the last words spoken when I left home. Even the long flight was good, knowing the war was over for seven days. I must have slept for at least ten hours of it.

Off the plane, girls ran out, and one threw a lei around my neck. It was an unexpected greeting of appreciation I thought, until she stuffed a card in my hand, if I cared to buy a picture of my friendly welcome. She then flashed off, took another lei from her arm and threw around another neck. It wasn't a total waste; I learned about crass commercialism and minor exploitation of our normal misery. I wasn't there for pretend welcomes. I didn't buy pictures.

I was quickly making my way to the civilian waiting area, eyes scanning faster than they ever did on patrol. With a big wave, Sherry came darting from the mass of wives, girl friends, and families - a vision that was hard to believe had arrived. All the days and nights of thinking about the moment disappeared as if they never happened.

My military duty started five days after our wedding. The local draft board, consisting of one woman, swatted away my request to leave with the next group of draftees a week or a month later. No doing, I would leave when I was told. I received my draft notice nine days before the wedding, too late to change plans on that end. We lived together a total of eight months the first two years of marriage. With my schedule, part of that time was barely better than living apart, as home was little more than a place to fall asleep for awhile before returning to duty.

We rushed from the airport to our hotel room. Sherry had made all arrangements and arrived at the hotel the prior day. We were a block from the beach and ten floors up; I think we were the only ones in the hotel. If others were there they weren't noticed. We had enough sexual energy stored that it was no less at the end of the seven days than it had been at the beginning, however we did find time to do other things.

War brought contemporary fame to Honolulu. Waikiki Beach and Diamond Head were icons already, but a local nightclub owner named Don Ho became an American household name and television's version of the Honolulu Police in *Hawaii Five-O* were cleaning up crime for several seasons.

"Is that Diamond Head?" I asked. Sitting on Waikiki seemed mandatory for us unworldly travelers. "It looks like the pictures, but I don't see the reason to call it Diamond Head; nothing diamond about it." Postcard photos of the whole scene were better than my observation. One trip wading out from the beach toward the rich blue Pacific water was enough. Before I got waist deep, I found sharp rock under the water, too sharp to walk across. I wrote off that frolicking image of Waikiki Beach then and there.

It was time to try surfing, where I found I was not a 'natural'. I was certain the guy rented me a board that wasn't waxed well, and hadn't enough how-to instructions. In the meantime, Sherry paddled too far out on a board, became exhausted and caught by the outgoing tide; she couldn't get back. She was rescued by the one native surfer who had gone out that far looking for a good wave. She still believes she would have ended up in Samoa or some similar place if he hadn't been out there to save her.

Another day we rented an open jeep with striped top and fringed edges to drive around the island. The two-lane road along the coast had hardly any traffic. We stopped along the way to watch breaking waves against the black, volcanic shore or spew water up through holes. A few photos and we were on our way, circling the inland toward the clouds. It was a great day, getting away from people, just us two together. It was a treat for me to drive a vehicle for the first time in six months. Other days were spent mostly in our hotel room.

In all the fun, when the quiet moments availed themselves, the platoon intruded into my thoughts. I wondered what they were doing, where they were, had I missed anything. It was the reversal of the thoughts I had while there, thinking of home any chance I got.

Don Ho's club was visited a couple of nights, consuming awful tasting drinks ordered by their color. I was not once asked for an ID. We discovered Black Angus steak houses, and I don't know how many times we ate there. I loved thick, juicy steaks. Those days were before beef was down- graded by the government to the current level. What is prime beef now was only choice then, and prime beef in 1968 was the most tender, melt-in-my-mouth taste imaginable. It seemed that we practically waited for the doors to open in the evenings as I made up for every can of ham and lima beans I had consumed the previous months.

The seven days ticked along. Time used or time remaining was not spoken of until the very end. I hated to go back but it was so much easier than leaving six months earlier. Half of my tour was finished, and I knew my days remaining in the field were limited; I had a much different frame of mind, yet that didn't put spring in my steps going back to the airport. A long goodbye was over, and the long flight back was boarded. I caught up on a week's sleep.

51

R&R was over. I asked the company clerk, "Where's the company now?" I expected them to be in a new location, but they weren't. They were still in the chicken barn on Highway 13. It took another day to catch transportation back to the field. It was late when I got there, and the platoon had already gone out for the night. That was good news to me since I wasn't anxious to spend my first day back on ambush; my mind hadn't cleared out thoughts of R&R yet. We had the next day off because of the ambush so there were two free Xs on my calendar. Each day counted when it came to an X.

"Yeah, R&R was great - what's been going on here?" There was nothing exciting to report. It was damn hot inside that metal building before afternoon clouds rolled in. It was hot and boring, and there were no adrenalin spikes from contact to alleviate either. I had a noticeable feeling that my return to the platoon brought a sense of comfort. It felt a little like going back home, not to be confused with my desire to get the hell out of there for my real home.

I was back on ambush the third night back. I had a higher sense of wariness that day. It wasn't a matter of being tentative as much as remembering I was on the home stretch, 'so don't screw up'. We left in mid-afternoon for a short patrol before moving on to our night position. I carried my VC poncho, a souvenir, in hope that it might stave off the inevitable rain. It was soft and pliable with a dull, matte finish, nicer than our own. I was envious that they could have such quality plastic, more suitable than our own equipment. It did rain, but it didn't keep me dry. Nothing kept us dry on ambush. I woke up off and on all night, chalking it up to my week of soft living in Hawaii.

We were radioed as soon as we got up the next morning to link up with the company for a sweep to the north. The sweep took us over an easy route, with room to spread out and plenty visibility.

The end of the operation was a rendezvous with an armor outfit, waiting in a light growth of brush and tall, slender palms. Not to let the occasion get away without firing on something, one of the tanks opened up with its fifty caliber machine gun. The fifty was my favorite weapon, considering fire rate, portability, range, and raw power. I'd fired one at Fort Benning during training, and fell in love. One round struck a skinny tree about fifty meters to his front. The four-inch diameter tree fell like an invisible chainsaw swept through as rounds ripped into vegetation, bits of leaves and limbs flipping in the air. The fun was over. It was time to go.

We gathered on a paved road too narrow for two vehicles to pass side-by-side. The company stretched out along the shoulders on both sides, mostly milling around, waiting on orders. I stood in my usual position, rifle slung over my shoulder, pistol grip in hand, letting the M-16 rest on pouches attached to my heavy pistol belt. Somewhere near the end of our operation, I unconsciously flicked the safety to off. My thumb was always on the safety switch as a habit. I stuck my finger inside the trigger guard, also not too unusual, and accidently popped off a single round. I'm sure my mouth flew open when I saw where the round hit. It was about six inches from Sergeant Potter's right boot. He stood on the opposite side of the road. I looked down then back up at him. He looked at me, speechless.

Five seconds later, Delta 6 was on the radio, "What's that firing?"

"... Accidental discharge, everything's okay."

I gave Potter an apologetic smile. "Sorry about that Sergeant Potter."

He never said a word, but was probably thinking of a few. Potter was special, terminally happy, laughing at something every day. He had recently returned from the States after serving one tour of duty with Delta Company, and requested to come back to the same company. Since we didn't need another squad leader at the time, we made him our company demolition man. He couldn't be happier than when blowing something up, causing a loud belly laugh so infectious it made everyone laugh with him. He had gained a lot of weight while in the States, but all the extra pounds were shed after humping in the heat for a few weeks.

We all had a good laugh later that day, about almost shooting him in the foot. "Shit, Potter, he was just trying to get you some time off in the rear. You need bigger feet." It gave the platoon something to laugh about, and humor was good.

That night would be our last in the barn. A new home awaited.

52

The choppers flew in and picked us up at 1330 hours. Other than the curiosity to see where our next NDP would be, I was in no hurry to leave the metal barn, certain the days of fresh French bread with C-ration lunches were over. Gone was the dry roof over my head, and an entire patrol area free of underbrush.

Instead of flying us all the way to our new NDP, which would have taken about two more minutes of flying time, we made an LZ three kilometers out. My platoon had insertion at the LZ and point the remainder of the way. It was a hot-as-hell day, as it always was with the sun out and carrying everything I owned. The reason for unloading us where they did escaped rational thought unless some prick planner at battalion operations believed a spare hour in the NDP may have ruined our day. The LZ was on the huge flat plain north of DiAn with nothing to see but low scrub and a few military trucks traveling up or down the paved highway in the distance. I'd seen enough of the area when we had our NDP nearby. There was no tactical reason for us to be there, and moving in full gear and rucksacks was ineffective in case of contact.

Humping along like a slug, I was glad to receive a radio message that the battalion LOH was coming to pick me up for an air recon of that night's ambush, which my platoon also had. It felt good to heave my rucksack aboard and fly away from the drudgery and heat.

Ambush was on the edge of the Dong Nai River which flowed south to Saigon. There was nothing but open ground at the coordinates given for the ambush. It didn't look very promising, but maybe we would get lucky. I hoped there was a good reason to send an ambush that far. With the recon finished, the chopper dropped me off at the new NDP which was already established just below the crest of a hill overlooking a large valley of rice paddies. The company First Sergeant was already there waiting. He had ridden out in his Jeep.

The platoon dragged in later with tired, blank looks on their faces that said "Fuck, what a stupid patrol." There was no time for them to start improving bunkers. The order was, "Drop your rucksacks, and everything else except ambush gear, and eat now if you're going to eat." It was another three klicks to the ambush site, and we had to leave two hours before dark to make it.

It was a slow and easy gait as we moved downhill toward the rice paddies. Our speed matched the tiredness and heat of the day. At the edge of the paddies, the platoon spread out, zigzagging its way across the skinny dikes for the most part of two kilometers. We dipped down through two of the gullies that ran through the valley floor, one shallow, the other wide and deep, but dry. It had yet to rain that day. It may have been three klicks by a straight line on the map, but the terrain and nearly constant changes of direction as we tacked back and forth across the dikes made it much further. Once out of the paddies, we crossed a narrow, paved highway. I had no idea where it went, but a few hundred meters to our right was a small ARVN compound guarding an equally small bridge. Another four or five hundred meters straight ahead was our destination. I could still see our NDP on the side of the hill, but it would have taken binoculars to see us, and there were none in the company. It seemed strange to have that kind of visibility. It was a first.

The ambush site didn't look any better at ground level than from the air. We did a quick early recon and moved in a little sooner than usual, under dark gray skies. No VC were coming near us unless they were in a boat on the river, but we were some distance from it. In fact, we couldn't see the water due to the riverbank vegetation. We were in short, sparse weeds without direct cover, but the river secured one side, and a small, steep-banked tributary perpendicular to the river secured another. There wasn't much way anyone could walk our way unless they were lost because there was no way to travel alongside the river. The platoon went about their well-rehearsed routine of setting out claymores.

In addition to the claymores, we had another piece of new technology   spikes that were pushed into the ground. They were listening devices, designed to hear footsteps through wired ear pieces. They were all but useless in the rainy season, as falling raining voided any other sounds.

In the midst of the activities I heard a small splash, then "Help...help... helllppp."

It sounded like a mouse trying to scream. I turned around, "What the fuck is going on over there?"

Somebody said, "It's Smith - he was putting out his claymore and slid down the bank." It was the near vertical, muddy bank of the small tributary feeding into the river.

"Well somebody drag his ass up." 'We should leave him down there all night,' was what I was thinking. It wasn't so dark that he couldn't see what he was doing, but it was the way he was every day; useless.

Private Smith was a recent addition to the field and was assigned to me, but I knew when I saw him that he was no prize. He might have weighed a hundred pounds with some of the black mud stuck to him, and he didn't know why he had been sent to the field either. I thought, 'Oh Lord, don't tell me they had somebody in the rear who was such a screw-up that he was sent to the field to get rid of him.'

"What's your MOS?" I asked him.

"Lineman."

"Lineman! You're not infantry?"

"No sir."

"Do you know anything about radios?"

"No sir, I was trained to install ground lines"

"What the fuck did they send you out here for? Jesus Christ - we don't use any land lines."

He just shrugged. "I don't know."

I told the CO as soon as I found out that he wasn't one of us and would like to send him some other place. I considered him a danger to the platoon and to himself, and didn't care where he went - just not in my platoon. The request was denied. He was given the job of RTO for one of the squads, thinking it would keep him out of the way. He got stuck in mud one day and it took two men to pull him out. That ended his RTO job.

After the water incident, I went back to the CO "...yes sir, went down the river bank. He doesn't know how to do anything right out here, and he's not strong enough to carry a radio. Besides that, he doesn't know anything about them either. I'm afraid he's going to get somebody hurt, and I have to have one man watching him all the time." I'd say anything to get rid of him, but it was all the truth. A couple of days later he was back in DiAn, working in the mess hall.

Rain started not long after dark. I had spent a lot of wet nights, and a number of them were cold and miserable for periods of time, but bearable. I was about to spend a night of misery unequaled in my life, before or since. I wrapped my poncho liner around me as usual, thinking the water would seal the tight nylon weave to help hold in body heat. It didn't. Neither did the rain stop as it eventually would on other nights.

I started shivering, unable to stop once I began, followed by teeth chattering until my whole body shook. I prayed for the rain to stop. I cursed. I tried moving my poncho liner slightly, thinking I didn't have it right and body heat was leaking out, but it made no difference. The rain was like ice darts striking hard. I could feel the individual drops hit my skin. It wasn't pouring, but it was constant. I couldn't smoke, which often relieved some misery. There was no way to get a cigarette lit. I was freezing and unable to move, unable to get my mind off the rain. 'I must be sick,' I thought. 'I've come down with something and the rain has knocked out my resistance.' There were almost nine hours until daylight, and I'd never experienced rain so cold and falling so long into the night. Sleep was impossible in the hypothermic conditions.

We were up and moving the next morning at the first crack of gray visibility, earlier than usual. We needed to get circulation going. I was wet and exhausted when we returned to the NDP. The mess tent was operating but ran out of food by the time I got to it. Dry clothes waiting for the platoon went a long way to help us return to a level of comfort. The day was spent constructing our bunker sleeping positions to be as dry as possible, but that was always a losing effort; with nothing more to use than our ponchos, leaks were a certain way of life.

#

I didn't want to think too far ahead, but it had entered my mind while we were moving the day before, that this could be my last NDP. The end of my time in the field was getting near, but there was no specific date. I didn't mention it to anyone, or dwell on it. It was better to take the days as they came.

53

I'd heard we had gotten a new Battalion Commander, and considered it good news without any other information about him. I wouldn't miss the old one. It seemed like he'd snuck in unannounced, but evidently there was no protocol for going around to see the new troops he was commanding. I never knew the reason why, but Captain Nolen met him once and hated him immediately. I thought it was more amusing than anything else, considering how mild-mannered the captain was, but when he called someone a son-of-a-bitch, you knew he was serious. Nothing ever made him curse, not even me.

If the captain hated him, the whole company had to hate him – it was as simple as that. The men liked Captain Nolen, and it was a matter of sticking together once word got around. I didn't know why the animosity with the CO, but he said one of his dislikes of the new colonel was the moustache. "He hates them," the captain said, as he started growing one. It was kind of reddish and not what I would have called fitting for him, but we weren't graded on beauty out there. When the captain started, the whole damn company started growing moustaches as a show of support. My growth didn't do much for my looks either, not that it mattered. Very few of the men could grow decent facial hair. It was like being on strike about something, only we didn't know what or why.

I got a chance to meet our new Commander, Lieutenant Colonel Gillis, a few days later at another of the colonel's personal quirks that the captain hated. He had a habit of inviting company officers to his command center for dinner. His headquarters was out on the flat plain back toward DiAn, and I couldn't believe what I saw hopping off the chopper. In front of his huge canvas tent sat a dining table complete with a white tablecloth and folding chairs. It looked like he was on a damn safari. I was smiling on the inside, but apprehensive about the new man until I met him.

I liked Colonel Gillis from the beginning, but first I admired him for setting up his headquarters in the field and living in a tent. I never knew our previous commander to spend any time in serious discomfort, except for the battalion-sized NDP we had for two weeks. I also thought our new colonel might be a wacky bastard, but a likeable kind. I considered him to be my kind of battalion commander.

While on patrol one day, he flew out in his LOH, landed and walked patrol with us. I was dumbfounded at the act, so accustomed to nothing but observation from above. Our patrol that day was back through the same brush-covered area that had the aggravating ground humps to maneuver around and through. The stiff-limbed brush constantly snagged gear and clothing alike. Movement was awkward with nearly every step. Colonel Gillis was walking along with me at the time and said, "It sure doesn't look like this from the air."

I smiled at him and thought 'Jesus, that's the biggest fucking understatement I've heard in six months,' but I said, "No sir, it's never very smooth down here."

Stumbling along, twisting to pass through some of the brush was a revelation to him, and I appreciated that he got on the ground to see what it was like. I never saw him again after that day, but before I left the field, the rumor going around was that he had ordered grass seed for his headquarters. "That bastard is crazy," the men said. I smiled and shook my head, but hoped it was true. He was one of a kind.

#

I had to find a new RTO. I looked around the platoon and decided on PFC Chapman. Brent Chapman, from Connecticut, turned out to be the closest thing I had to a friend while in the field, whether he realized it or not. We constantly sat around talking about our lives back in the States. He was kind of a silly bastard, always doing some nonsense in the NDP like walking around with only one pant leg rolled up or parting his hair down the middle to match his well-groomed moustache.

We got along fine until one rainy night on ambush. We huddled close together on the rain nights, to combine our two poncho liners for more effective coverage and warmth. Placed just right, we could have two layers of nylon over parts of us, a definite help in battling the effects of cold rain. One night I pulled both liners around me while sleeping, and he couldn't get his back. He was duly pissed-off the next morning, declaring, "I won't be sharing poncho liners anymore." I had no memory of it and apologized. Our relationship was still perfect afterward, but we never shared our poncho liners again.

#

I needed a new point man for the platoon. Palmer had given up the job and I'd rotated several men on point, hoping to find one that both liked it and was good at it. It wasn't a job that men were itching to take, and finally I had to tell the squad leaders to pick one of their own men on days that their particular squad was on point. I was still trying to recruit one, and didn't like forcing the job. We were in the perfect place to break in a new man, with so much open territory. Almost the whole platoon could see where we were headed at any given time, unlike busting through heavy crap, blind beyond ten feet.

I thought we had the perfect man in Private Kuality. We called him Tonto simply because he was an American Indian from Oklahoma. He even looked like he should be a good point man. I had based my high opinion of his potential abilities on what I'd seen about Indians on television, since I had never been west of the Mississippi River. He hadn't been in the field a long time, and I finally talked him into giving it a try. "It's a piece of cake - you'll probably like it." We broke him in slowly, no pressure, on easy patrols.

We were traveling over soft rolling hills, vegetation no higher than our boots, but he would hesitate every couple of hundred yards with a question or verification about something. It was a sign that he was spooked, and I knew it. During one of his pauses, I walked to his position, whistling. I stopped when I got to him. "What's up?' It was on his face. He wasn't a point man.

He was a nice guy, quiet and likeable, but he couldn't take it on the point, so I walked along with him for a while. He didn't have to do it again. A few days later I was talking to him; as I went around the bunkers to bullshit a little with the men, he told me that he couldn't believe I was whistling when I walked up to him. I did it intentionally, hoping to relax him, but when he mentioned it to me later I realized how unsuitable he was for the job. I had failed in my estimation that Indians had the innate instinct for that kind of job. He was just like me. It was an unfortunate blow soon afterward when he received a 'Dear John' letter from his wife. She wanted a divorce.

54

Sitting up on that hill was a good life. Panoramic views extended for kilometers. The sweep of rice paddies full of water flickering in the morning sun was a mosaic of flashing signal mirrors contained by thin, green borders. It was by far the best place I'd been in nearly six months, and I was relaxed as if there was no war anywhere near. I knew that I was a short-timer in the field. I was very near the six-month mark and that was as long as officers, regardless of rank, served in the field.

#

Patrol days turned out to be rare. In an eleven day period, seven of the nights were spent on ambushes. We had one rainless night. The others were either cold rain, or we were soaked from pre-dark rain that allowed the mosquitoes to move in on us. Some ambushes were as close as four-hundred meters out, others two-and-a-half kilometers, some in between.

The nights were generally as quiet as the days. Third platoon saw two VC one night but not close enough to engage, and battalion headquarters received a rocket attack the same night, but it was well off target.

#

The first platoon had one man shot in the chest by accident one evening. They were setting up an ambush on a low rising hill about a thousand yards, a kilometer, or less from a small ARVN outpost down below our NDP. The handful of soldiers there wildly fired a few rounds in the air every evening before they left for their village. One of the rounds hit one of our men. He lived, luckily.

#

Our second night took us on an ambush across the small bridge guarded by that same ARVN outpost during the day, up near the village on the hillside above it. This was before the day that one of them shot the man in first platoon. We sat beside the dirt and rock cart road below the village, waiting later than usual before moving into our graveyard site for the night. Since there were people nearby, I wanted absolute cover of darkness before our final positioning; somebody would be watching us and I didn't care what the reason.

A lone, small boy came up the road driving a few head of cattle toward the village, but it was right at dark - curfew time. Out much later than he should be, he aroused my suspicion, old enough to tip off someone about our presence. We waited until he passed before moving.

We had hardly gotten our claymores set out and settled down when explosions started hitting beyond our positions. There was no mistaking the sound of an M-79 grenade launcher. We could hear the 'thump' sound on firing. The exploding shells were also familiar. I called in to the captain.

227

"Delta 6, Delta 6, this is November 6 ... we are receiving 40mm grenade rounds. It sounds like they are coming from the backside of the village. There is no way we can return fire."

Captain Nolen asked, "How close are they hitting?"

"Right now they are right over our heads hitting maybe thirty meters behind us." That night, we had better than normal protection offered by the graveyard. Every one of my men was lying inside the low walls that surrounded individual graves.

"Can you hold off and not fire into the village?"

"Roger, as long as they don't get any closer." There was a limit to our silence. Persistence on their part to keep firing would have brought return fire from our own grenade launcher, village or no village.

The incoming stopped. I didn't believe it was VC; I doubted they would have an M-79. It was more likely the same ARVN's who fired from the small bridge every evening, but it made no difference to me. I didn't know them, and they could have been VC sympathizers as far as I knew. Firing on us was enemy action as far as I was concerned.

Back at the NDP the next morning, the captain thanked me for keeping calm the night before. I was more mad that we didn't have a clear firing sector toward them than I was calm. All field units were already under a no-fire or limited-fire order that clearly came from a political decision in Washington. We were not allow to fire unless we had received fire and had a clear target. I believe it was part of the political pacification strategy at the time, to win the hearts and minds of the general population. If we received fire from a village or populated area, we were not to return fire unless we had clearance from battalion headquarters, after it coordinated with the Vietnamese District Headquarter for permission to fire. A lot of grumbling went on when the men heard the new restrictions, but it was our opinion that we would say screw no-fire zones if we received fire, then accept the consequences if necessary.

#

The luck of the draw in ambush rotations sent my platoon back to the same place we had the first night in wretched, cold rain; it was the farthest distance from the NDP of any ambush. I hated that particular long one only because we had to leave so early to get there. It was the same long trip back the next morning. The round trip out and back could be three hours or more.

As with the first day, our small tribe of a platoon slipped east, away from the NDP, down the lower side of the hill into the rice paddies. It had rained earlier, and the paddies were filled to the tops of their dikes; the deep gully running through the valley that we had slid into and climbed up the other side of earlier was full and running strong with monsoon runoff. We had the required rope to get a swimmer across, then the platoon cross hand-over-hand, only heads above rushing, muddy water. The process added another thirty minutes to our travel time. Two helmets and a rifle were lost to the water during the crossing. Every step was a miserable trek toward the Dong Nai River.

The first platoon left the NDP an hour after us, for an ambush about a kilometer out. They crossed the same gully, a few hundred meters upstream from us, at a place no more than waist-deep.

We had already made our water crossing when we heard their radio call, "... Delta 6, this is Lima 6, we are covered with leeches and request to abort the ambush and return to base."

The CO gave them the okay; I was stunned that they asked such a question, and more so by the fact that they were allowed to return. It was like a slap to the face of our whole platoon. We had over twice as far to travel and under much more difficult conditions.

"Can you believe that bunch of panty-waist ribbon clerks asking to go back to get leeches off. Shit, they could have done that when they got to their ambush site. Jesus, I can't believe that bunch of chicken-shits. Fucking leeches? They couldn't take the fucking leeches?" The sarcastic ranting continued. "What the hell would they have done if they had drawn our ambush? Jesus, I can't fucking believe they're going back, the sorry-ass bastards." It made me think, 'Do they not have any pride in their job? Living and working in shit conditions is part of it, and we all do it without asking to please not send me here or there. They are a fucking disgrace to the company and the Infantry in general, pulling crap like that.'

The veteran members of our platoon were outraged that the first platoon had the easiest mission possible, and that it was stopped by leeches. Leeches had never been anything to stop and worry about. They were impossible to feel when they were on us anyway, never more than nuisances removed during breaks or after returning from patrol.

We crossed the rest of the paddies still pissed off about Lima platoon. Movement had been so slow that we had only reached the narrow paved highway by dark, a few hundred meters short of our destination by the Dong Nai River. I'd allowed for extra time by leaving early, but we were still behind schedule.

A permanent, platoon-sized ARVN compound that protected the bridge was no more than a couple of hundred meters to our right, I figured. One of my men was posted there as a mortar forward observer for our company. The captain asked me to supply a man for the job the day we arrived. It was a great assignment. It meant no patrols or ambushes, and it wasn't difficult to get a yes when I asked one of the men to be stationed there full-time. I had a good man there, Sergeant Delap, as I remember. He had a company radio and a call sign in case he needed to direct mortar fire.

I decided it was time to do something tricky, if not potentially dangerous. Democracy and the military were not in the same universe, even further apart in the field, but I had mellowed after six months. The platoon gathered on the pavement. We were wet from the neck down and there was no need to rush anywhere; it was already pitch black and time didn't mean much anymore. I got the squad leaders together, and laid out a question for the platoon to vote, although I felt I could predict the outcome.

"Listen up, we can either go on to the ambush site, or we can go down the road to the ARVN compound, see if we can contact Sergeant Delap and spend the night in there. Hell, we might need to check and see if we have leeches too," added in ridicule of the first platoon. I never asked permission to change orders in the field. I knew the rules, and if I broke them I was ready to accept responsibility if we got caught.

As expected, the platoon thought the compound was a good idea. Since I was soon to leave the field, I didn't worry about setting a precedent for poor discipline as much as rewarding the platoon for all the haranguing I had put some of them through the last few months. The new men may not have understood, but others could see I had a side that wasn't by the book all the time.

Making the decision was the easy part. How to make contact with our man, without alerting other radios listening-in within the company, or getting shot by the Vietnamese soldiers was the trick. First, I tried contact by radio under the pretext of letting him know we were in the area, to get out on the wire and tell the ARVN's not to fire at any sound they may hear in the next few minutes.

"Shit, he's not answering his radio." I kept calling and cursing for a couple of minutes but got nothing.

My contingency plan was less desirable, and a lot scarier. It involved moving toward the compound, calling out, hoping some trigger-happy little bastards didn't open up on us; I envisioned what could easily go wrong in the blackness. The platoon spread out and dropped down while two or three of us quietly moved along the road, calling out somewhere between a loud whisper and a low yell, "Sergeant Delap! Sergeant Delap!" I didn't know how far away we were. I also didn't want to walk right upon their perimeter and hit a trip wire. It was a spooky situation even if it was only friendlies involved. Bullets were bullets and they didn't care whose weapon they came from. We moved and yelled every two or three steps in the purest "American" voice we could. 'Surely they can recognize accents,' I thought. I held my breath after every call. 'Please don't let them shoot us.' I had begun to regret the whole idea.

"Who's that?" Sergeant Delap called out.

The compound was small, but large enough to accommodate my platoon. I explained to Delap our change in plans as one of the command decisions we have to make from time to time, and made sure word of it never got out. Field expedience it was called.

"Yes, they wanted to open fire, but thought it may be American voices. They came and got me. You were probably lucky," he said. There was no doubt that we were.

We were up and gone by half-light, slithering our way back across the paddies. Immediately after breakfast, we had to make a trip back to the gully to retrieve the lost items, but we had the day off and the mood was light. Not a trickle flowed down the gully that morning, as it waited on the next flash flood to refill. The two steel helmets and rifle lay in the bottom mud near the spot they were dropped.

#

The next night our ambush was only four hundred meters out. It was my last one. The following morning, I was informed my field time was over, and Sergeant Potter was put in command of the platoon. I had no more ambushes, no patrols, no miserably cold rain to endure. I felt a little guilty about leaving, knowing the platoon's life wouldn't change. It was a low key exit. I went into DiAn to start signing over papers as Delta Company's new XO. I was out of the field, a REMF - just like that. I thought it would be the perfect job; sometimes though, I was wrong on my thinking.

55

The rear provided an immediate decompression from the field that I couldn't have anticipated in advance. It was such a new life, a hundred and eighty degrees from before. I relaxed and absorbed the mental and physical solitude to my core as soon as I arrived, no briefings, no patrol or ambush duty. If there was a schedule to go by, I paid no attention to it. I had time to burn.

My top priority was a trip to battalion supply to find a few sets of decent-looking fatigues. I wanted fatigues that fit, with matching shirts and pants. I wanted our division shoulder patch on every shirt. In the field we got shirts dropped by supply that were often missing patches, and everybody scrambled around to find ones with the Big Red One patch. It didn't matter if we were the only ones who would see them. The importance of the patch in the boonies seemed strange, but that was pride of being in the First Division.

I hoarded as many pairs of socks as supply would part with then looked through the bin and found a nicer pair of boots. They weren't new or shiny, but they were still black instead of looking like brown suede once the black leather was worn away. I looked good I thought, more like a human being but no doubt still a grunt. I got sets of name tags in black, heavily embroidered letters sewn on my shirts, along with rank. I had transformed into a REMF, but the kind that infantry aspired to become. I had put my time in the field first. I was 'a strack soldier' as we would say in mock compliments.

#

A freight train called boredom was fast coming. The simple fact was that it didn't take long to find out I didn't like it in the rear. It was too quiet. Since I had a jeep, and the NDP was a few miles up the road, I spent each day of the next week back out in the field. I was only visiting, but I was comfortable sitting in the NDP, a bird set free only to return. I had no business to take care of in the rear; the daily administrative paperwork was handled by the company clerk, and I had no daily function. I wondered what other Executive Officers did in the rear before me. There were no briefing as to what my job would be other than make sure free refreshments were on hand when the company came in from the field.

Maybe I went back out because I knew I was immune to that walk through the wire, no patrol or ambush. I could go back into DiAn where I had a bunk, a dry roof overhead, and warm showers anytime I wanted. I had an entire building to myself when the company was in the field, and they seldom came to the rear. I no longer slept under a leaky poncho roof with four of us stretched out in a five-by-twelve foot space. The war with mosquitoes, mud, rain, and exhaustion was over; only boredom remained.

#

Delta Company's fourth platoon was the weapons platoon, made up of three 81mm mortars. The platoon leader had cycled out of the field well before me. After a few days in the rear, I asked Captain Nolen if I could take over that platoon at least until they got a replacement. I thought surely somebody would be happy to have a volunteer for the field.

I trained and qualified on mortars in the fall and winter of 1966 at Fort Dix, New Jersey, before I went to OCS. It was weeks of miserable training on the treeless, windswept mortar range in near freezing weather, unable to wear gloves while manipulating sights and settings.

The mortar platoon went on patrol or ambush only when the company was humping to a new NDP, which was acceptable to me. The captain said 'no' without explanation. I felt like I had been kicked out of the club, and they wouldn't let me back in.

My replacement for November platoon showed up about a week after I left. I had enjoyed my daily visits back at the platoon with Sergeant Potter and Chapman, my old RTO, and some of the men, just to sit and shoot the shit when they weren't on patrol, but decided I'd best end it when their new man arrived. I met him and gave him a brief rundown on the platoon, which men he could count on to get the job done. Three weeks later, he stepped in a hole and sprained his ankle. I had spent months stumbling, tripping, stepping in things, often going to one knee to get up and keep going, and nothing, never close to hurting myself. He spent weeks recuperating.

#

I was soon joined by some company. Spec 4. Armstrong had been in my platoon and was also from Nashville. He got promoted to REMF status as company Jeep driver, and I was glad it was him. I expected he was chosen the usual way; besides doing a good job in the field, he was married and had kids. It was a chance to make life easier for his family. Things like that were taken into consideration when there was a job opening in the rear.

I liked him, and we had enough in common to always have things to talk about. Once our wives found out there were two of us from Nashville, they got together and shared photo slides and information received in letters home. I laughed every time he got out his letter writing kit. He kept his paper and pens stored in one of his kids' beat up tin lunch boxes with cowboys and Indians on it.

\#

We were the only two to live in our platoon's barrack and had our own small generator for lights and any other electrical luxuries that could be rounded up. Armstrong took care of firing it up in the evenings and keeping it full of gas. One night it quit and no amount of tapping, looking, and yanking on the starter rope brought it back to life.

"Well shit, we're done now until we find somebody that can fix this thing," was my interpretation of the situation.

"Stay here, I'll go get the jeep." He was back soon with the jeep parked around back of our building.

"Here, let's get this thing un-wired and up on the back of the jeep." I thought maybe he knew somebody who could fix it, but that wasn't his plan at all.

"What're you going to do?"

"Hop in, and I'll show you - we'll swap this for another one."

"Good," I said, mistakenly thinking there was a place we could take it to exchange for one that worked. I learned better in about a minute.

We began our journey by getting out of our company area. We rode around slowly, looking for an unlit, vacant building with a generator sitting outside. That was an easy task with troops always in the field. We quickly made the swap, even hooking up the wiring on the broken generator to avoid suspicion. That's how broken equipment got fixed.

The local acquisition technique went well beyond generators. It was best to keep anything you wanted locked up. Armstrong kept a logging chain and lock handy to insure our jeep stayed where we left it. Even midday at the PX, floor pedals and the steering wheel all had to be bound together with the chain and locked to make sure it was there when we got back. Otherwise it would be found at the other side of the base, or never found at all.

#

Plans for each day were decided sometime after I got up. One morning I went to the 93rd Evac Hospital to check on the man who got shot by the ARVN's near the NDP while he was setting up on ambush.

"Hey Lieutenant, you want to see my scar?" he asked with pride. Grunts were proud of scars.

"Yeah, what does it look like?" He opened his hospital gown. "Jesus Christ, I didn't know you were hit that bad." He had been hit dead center of his lower chest, and a long scar ran down the center of his body to his abdomen, in near perfect symmetry.

"Yeah, the bullet hit something inside and ricocheted downward. The only way the doctors could follow the path and look for all the damage was to open me up wherever it traveled." He was smiling.

#

Another day, I chauffeured a couple of our men to the 90th Replacement Company at Long Binh. They were on top of the world, going home. Smiles went all around, good lucks were said, and we were off. That was the extent of my job.

I discovered there was a USO in DiAn just outside the South gate. DiAn was the small rural town that was the namesake for our base. I had never seen a USO. It was incredible to me that there was one there, in an old building outside the gate, and it was packed. I thought, 'What a target this place would make.' It looked like every REMF from DiAn base camp was in there. The hamburger I ate said nothing but homemade America, nothing foreign, nothing military, but I never went back. It was something about the crowd and noise. I didn't belong there.

#

We had our own one-room Battalion Officer's Club. It was nothing more than a bar, with a connecting mess hall where everyone ate in the next room. The club was little used but it was open every day. I was the only one in the bar every afternoon. It opened at around1600 hours. By my logic, if it was open, it was alright to use, and it easily became a daily ritual. By the time I swung around off the barstool one afternoon to go in eat, they had already finished serving and cleaned up the mess hall. It was hard to believe I drank dinner, sitting in the next room with the door open.

The bar made life in the rear much more tolerable, but it also allowed me to skew my judgment. I was walking to the barrack at dusk one evening, half-plastered, my M-16 slung on my shoulder. I saw a small snake in a large grass field. I un-slung my rifle, locked and loaded, put the muzzle about two inches from the ground and fired. Bang! No more snake. I looked up and around. Every man in the surrounding buildings was either in the door or outside staring. I yelled, "Snake," and walked off. I had forgotten, but it was against regulations to have a weapon chambered, much less fire one, inside the wire in DiAn. Later, I was thinking I would probably be standing in front of some colonel's desk explaining what the hell I was doing, but I never heard a word.

#

My tenure as Executive Officer lasted fifteen days when notification came that I would be transferring to a job at 2d Brigade Headquarters. I didn't like the job of XO and was elated at the news. I was a little curious as to whether battalion was getting rid of me for reasons of unsavory conduct in the rear, or if by luck, the wheel was spun and the big needle landed on my name. It made no difference to me; my bag was packed in a flash.

56

Lieutenant Mike DeGarmo was going home in a couple of weeks. I knew him earlier when he was the mortar platoon leader in Delta Company, but lost track of where he'd gone after leaving the field. I never knew how or why I became his replacement, but however the job came about, I was the lucky winner with the result. It was an assignment of substance, something more than the glorified office clerk I was as XO.

Improvement Action Team, IMPACT for short, was the official name of my new group and was located in brigade headquarters. It was a three-man team: me, an enlisted man, and a Vietnamese interpreter. Our geographic scope spread over the five districts within the 2nd Brigade AO (area of operation), each about the size of a small county back home. Its function was to serve as advisory and assistance to Vietnamese district operations. Exactly what that meant I didn't know.

DeGarmo and I headed out in the jeep on my first full day to visit each of the district headquarters. I wanted to see their locations and introduce myself, fulfilling the formality of the new job.

We visited four of them. The last one that afternoon was Tan Uyen in the furthermost northeast corner of our AO. Driving up a narrow paved highway allowed the only southern access. The road was flat and ran parallel with the Dong Nai River along our right side.

"Hey, yeah, I know where we are now. Delta was up on that hill when I left the field," pointing to our left across the paddies. I recognized the section of road when we crossed the bridge protected by the small triangular ARVN compound. "One of my men pulled duty as the company's mortar forward observer when we were out here" I told DeGarmo. I didn't mention it was also the place where my platoon spent a night, instead of on our ambush site after we got pissed-off about the other platoon aborting their ambush because of leeches.

The narrow highway was hardly wide enough for two large vehicles to pass in opposite directions, but we hadn't seen traffic on it that day. I seldom saw any vehicles other than military trucks going to and from the compound when I was up on the hill across the shallow valley.

Not far beyond the bridge we drove upon an engineer unit – an odd occurrence, I thought, see out in nowhere, especially without the usual heavy earth-moving equipment. One man stood in the road and flagged us down.

"What are you guys doing out here?" DeGarmo asked, indicating they appeared to be out of their element. There was no heavy equipment visible or work going on.

"They're up there blowing mines, sir. You might not want to drive up that way today." He didn't know the type of mine or how they were set, but he knew that's what they were doing out there, and that was good enough for us. We agreed with his recommendation and turned around. It wasn't critical that we get there, and in fact I never once went to Tan Uyen.

#

A large, well defined map of the districts overlaid with acetate hung on the wall beside my new desk. It was pockmarked like artillery strikes, with more than a hundred colored push pins stuck in it. Each pin represented a South Vietnamese military installation of some sort.

I studied the map, disregarding the pins, but trying to recognize various places I had operated in the last six months. I had never seen a map of our complete area of operations, always concerned only with areas often no greater than fifty square kilometers, when in the field, depending on location and terrain. I looked for familiar landmarks, cart road intersections or villages I may have seen on patrols. I could recall many patrol routes and ambush sites in both the Thu Duc district and the region north of DiAn.

"I have the pins color-coded for the most part," Mike said. "I never made it around to all of them. Some locations may no longer exist, or there may be new ones not on the map."

"I can see why you didn't get to all of them. That's a lot of pins."

"The places I've been have different color pins depending on how large the place is." He explained how blue, red, and white pins represented different security types and sizes. "Some are no more than a two-man daytime guard post, and others are full time fortified locations. Some locations are more important than others, but they're mostly to the south, around Thu Duc to the river at Saigon." The security of that region was the main focus of my work for the next few months.

The pins on the map provided a way to spend slack time in future days. Without bona fide work to do, which was frequently the case, I picked various pins' locations to go to in the jeep and searched for their existence. It was hardly more than an amusing scavenger hunt, but I did learn where and how the Vietnamese operated their security. On the whole, they received little equipment from their government, and they never failed to appreciate whatever I could furnish them in the way of defensive materials.

#

My new boss was Major Joe Taitano, in charge of the Brigade S-5 section. They took care of Psychological Operations and reimbursements to civilians for crop and animal damages caused by soldiers. Technically, I belonged in the S-3 which was the Operations department.

The problem was that S-3's physical space was full to the seams with its primary operations, and we weren't an integral part of those. Consequently, the team function had been transferred to Major Taitano in S-5, and he never appreciated it. I was an orphan of sorts.

He informed me soon after my arrival that he didn't want to know what I was up to every minute, in a way I interpreted as, "I don't know what you do and don't care. Just find something to stay busy every day." It wasn't directed at me personally, but the IMPACT team.

Although I made a couple of my own missteps, the major and I had a pleasant, good working relationship. As I, he didn't believe in bullshit with anyone. I liked the major, and we got along perfectly fine.

A native Hawaiian, he was tall, slender, had an even temperament, and spoke only when and as much as he needed. He was known by those of us in lesser ranks as 'Surfer Joe' and was a skilled regular in our evening game of physical contact combat volleyball. He had also served in the Special Forces which I didn't find out until later, when I had my own experiences with the Green Berets.

#

Our office building was roughly the same size as a platoon's barrack. It was unpainted wood clapboard with a screen door on each end. Only six people worked there. The building sat on the semicircular front drive, next door to the brigade headquarters building.

Two other team operations shared the same building, the PsyOps and the office that paid for damage claims. If a villager's water buffalo was killed, or crops damaged by soldiers, they filed a claim and were reimbursed for their losses.

Our three disparate departments thrown together in one building made an odd lot with nothing in common. I was occasionally asked, "What do you people do over there?" It made me feel special that my job, with its ability to move around freely every day without broadcasting our mission, was far above the average REMF's job; it never hurt to have a mystery.

The PsyOps was the best job anywhere. They made leaflets to drop from choppers with surrender instructions for the Viet Cong. They also made taped recordings. The recordings were played at night from large loud speakers mounted beneath a chopper as it flew around suspected VC areas broadcasting messages to surrender.

After I had been there for several months, I thought it would be fun to go up on the Psy-Op chopper to ride around in the dark. The lieutenant who ran the section didn't care. Since it would take place after my duty hours, I nonchalantly announced the plan to the Major. "I'm going up with the PsyOps chopper tonight."

"No, you're not," was the reply in a calm tone of concrete certainty. Although mildly stunned and irritated about him vetoing my fun, after some thought I was convinced he was thinking of my safety, by possibly avoiding my unfortunate demise in the low-flying chopper. The VC were known to be superstitious and in theory they would think the recorded sounds were dead ancestors urging them to surrender, which would have made them the most superstitious and gullible enemy ever encountered. The less gullible of them were known to take a few shots at the chopper.

#

Mike DeGarmo was one of those eternally cheerful people, upbeat and smiling regardless of what he was talking about. He was also the most easily spooked person I had ever seen when he got really short. Worse than superstitious, he was certain that an errant incoming rocket or mortar round had his name on it. After my first few days there, he was finished with everything except the last ride to 90th Replacement. He quit going outside the wire at DiAn, and we laughed that he probably slept under his bunk with his helmet on.

It was nice for me to personally give him a hard time as a chicken-shit short-timer. Some few months earlier, in Delta Company we were in the rear and had the rare opportunity to all sit at a table and eat. The company's lieutenants sat together at one table, the singular time that happened, eating and talking when close explosions started. Before the echo of the first sound left, I had already slapped the edge of the table and pushed my chair back, headed under the table. They all looked down the table at me and burst out laughing, "Hey, where you going?" It was terribly amusing to them, causing a sheepish look on my face. I was the only one that didn't know a 4.2 (four-point-two) inch mortar battery had set up across the street, less than a hundred feet from where we were eating. The big mortars were essentially the same size and noise level as a 107mm. howitzer.

I took him down one afternoon to catch his flight home. He was literally shaking. He had to spend his last night in-country, his last wake-up, at the 90th Replacement. That night the huge munitions depot at Bien Hoa received a rocket attack. One rocket had a direct hit inside one of the high-bermed containment compartments of explosives. We could see the red sky miles away in DiAn, and everyone laughed about DeGarmo, what he was going through mentally, probably less than a mile away from the explosions. We hoped he was near a medic and a bunker.

57

"Yes Sir, I'll get right on it." My first official job involved dirt. I didn't know where the order came from but Major Taitano told me where it went and said "Take care of it."

I was relieved that my sergeant knew where to get a load of dirt. B Company, 1st Engineer Battalion was stationed on the far side of DiAn from our headquarters. We made a direct run to the engineers. I introduced myself and explained my team, not knowing then how involved the engineers would be in my immediate future, or how they would learn to dread the sight of me pulling up in front of their headquarters. I'm sure to them I was no more than an official scrounger inventorying their supplies to see what I could give away.

"I need a truck load of dirt." It was going to a bridge south of Thu Duc, toward Saigon. I showed them the location on a map. No requisitions were required; that alone was unmilitary-like, and I liked it. I hated paperwork.

The time I spent with DeGarmo was spent doing nothing more than riding around to different places, but no real work. I'm not even positive that he did any tangible work with supplies. I liked the physical work, and that morning got me to the bones of the job.

I didn't know the bridge, so we made a quick recon in the Jeep to check it out and see what was going on. Under layers of rust and flaking paint stood an old, iron suspension bridge that had seen better days. It reminded me of the old iron bridges crossing creeks and small rivers I knew back home. A large section of the paved two-lane across it had been reduced to one lane, and patched with timbers from an earlier VC attack. Located on a back road connecting Thu Duc and Saigon, it was a long way from a first class bridge, but it was important both tactically and for local traffic.

A large tributary flowed a few meters below, near the confluence of the Dong Nai and Saigon Rivers. The location was manned by a full time ARVN contingent. The first thing I noticed was the sandbagged machine gun bunker covered by a low, corrugated tin roof at the highest point above the highway. It sat on the transverse steel beams connecting the sides.

The ARVN soldiers were making improvements for security for both themselves and the bridge. Their fortifications and camp were on the south side of the bridge. I didn't have an interpreter that day, and communication was a haphazard game of charades; by the time we left, I thought they understood that the dirt was on the way. They had bales of sandbags waiting to fill.

We drove back up the road to Thu Duc district headquarters to let them know what we were doing down the road and to kill time waiting on the delivery.

That was the place I met Lieutenant-Colonel Gallagher. I had no idea who he was, or that I would become closer to him than anyone else for the remainder of my time in-country. He was the assistant brigade commander. It was an unexpected moment by any measure, and a flash of discomforting wariness came over me. It was a built-in suspicion I had developed for high ranks. I feared he may be some gung-ho colonel similar to the first battalion commander I had there - always planning something to enhance his career, regardless of necessity. To me, it wasn't a good sign to see the assistant brigade commander out making rounds in his jeep. My thoughts of running an independent operation, free of constantly examining eyes, disappeared.

"Did you take care of that dirt this morning?" The colonel had a relaxed, easy manner in his question, directly opposite of the impression I took from his appearance.

"Yes sir, I did. The engineers will have it there by afternoon." He knew exactly what I was doing that day before he asked the question. He was my real boss, probably the originator of the order from Major Taitano. I just didn't know it immediately. From that point on, I worked directly for the colonel any time there was an important project to handle.

He had been around the military a long time, judging by his age and general fitness. It had been years since he had done push-ups or the mile run. Average height and mildly rotund, he lacked, or preferred to dispense with, the spit-shine, gung-ho attitude of the young commanders of equal rank. He was a gentle old bull. If I had known then what a mentor was, he would have been mine. My initial concerns couldn't have been more misplaced.

#

It was difficult for me to be relaxed around superior officers. If at all possible, I chose anonymity. My time and experience in the Army had very little place for socialized behavior with upper grade officers. As a freshly commissioned lieutenant at Fort Campbell, Kentucky, my wife and I had been invited to a battalion officers' cocktail party at my battalion commander's home. Spit-shined in dress greens and stiff with fear, I dropped the white calling card with my name onto the small silver tray inside the front door. It was required protocol.

Beyond introduction, I managed to avoid the major, but his southern wife was very charming and easy to carry on a conversation with. I complimented her on the hors' d'oeuvres, especially the Swedish meatballs, a sophistication of high cuisine in my twenty-year-old mind and palate. I couldn't stop singling them out as the most delicious thing until she told me they were the only dish that she didn't personally prepare. I became frozen, unable to speak after such an insult, sure my face was red. I knew I was dead when she told the major, but she burst out laughing, most likely at my state of discomfort while trying to get enough apologies out of my mouth.

#

Lieutenant-Colonel Gallagher was different from anyone else I had ever worked for in the Army. He had a steady gait, never excited, rushed, or overly concerned about work, but professional at all times. Maybe because I gave him no reason, he never raised his voice or expressed any criticism during our months together. He had a slight chuckle at humorous or ironic moments.

Each time I offered an obstacle to a job with, "Sir, I don't think we can do that," he always had one answer - "You wanna bet?" Before long he was known in my heart as 'You Wannabet Gallagher', because I knew his words before they left his mouth.

After several weeks on the job, the colonel gave me something to do that I knew was impossible; the engineers said no to my request. I had seriously reduced their inventory in some areas and would drive by their storage yard to survey the stocks and recent deliveries. Doing that, I knew what they had before I asked for something. I loved to see new shipments of concertina wire stacked high; I would be back a day or two later with a trailer to take a few rolls for some small outpost.

Lieutenants held a low threshold of authority, and the given job was beyond my pay grade. Upon explanation of the refusal, the familiar gravelly words came out of his mouth, "You wanna bet?" along with raised eyebrows.

"Sir, there are things a lieutenant colonel can do that a first lieutenant can't do." I had been waiting on that opportune moment for awhile. He smiled; I had made an understatement of grand proportion. I suspected he took delight in the prospect of jumping on somebody's ass about giving me a hard time. He carried tremendous power as assistant commander. I was the colonel's boy; from then on I had little trouble.

#

We rode back to the bridge later than afternoon to check on the delivery. The dirt was there. It had been dumped at the north end of the bridge, and the ARVN's little compound was on the opposite side of the river. The dump truck couldn't have made it across that patchwork of timbers.

"We will be back in the morning." That was the best I could tell them at the moment. The soldiers had attacked the dirt pile with considerable enthusiasm, setting filled bags to the side. Their problem was getting the filled bags across the bridge. They would have been more than grateful for a wheelbarrow or a cart, but they had nothing. The filled bags were heavy to transport one at a time on their shoulders.

I returned the next morning with the jeep, and they piled the hood with filled bags until it had half-flat tires. They were driven across the bridge and down the river bank to their compound and the jeep returned for another load. We helped them for two days and they were overjoyed to have the help.

The sandbags were used to enclose a small steel conex shipping container they had gotten for a bunker. I thought walls one bag thick was enough, but there was an old sergeant who would have none of it. In a rather animated argument in sign language, he finally yanked up his shirt to show me the scars on his body from RPG shrapnel. To stop RPGs, he insisted the walls must be two bags thick. I didn't argue any more.

58

"Go find us a trailer for the jeep, Rodgers." He was my new driver and was back in a few minutes. We were on to our new mission.

Lieutenant-Colonel Gallagher had briefed me the evening before that I would be providing transportation for a Special Forces Team. They turned out to be a scuba team. Orders came down from Division Headquarters with a list of major bridges in our AO that would undergo an underwater survey of fortifications, primarily concertina wire, and they were the inspectors. I thought it was probably precautionary work in case there might be any form of another offensive like Tet a year earlier. The bridge pilings had to be safe from access by sappers' explosives.

The team consisted of two men plus their equipment; air tanks, fins, masks, and other paraphernalia were thrown in the trailer. "Which one do you want to check first?" It made no difference to me. It was their show, and I served no active part of the job, other than transportation.

"Let's start with the Newport, get it out of the way, since it's the largest," the team leader said. Light tension existed between us at the beginning, no doubt because we came from different tribes, indicated by the shoulder patches we wore. I wore the Big Red One, and they wore the 5th Special Forces. I suspect it was a natural reaction until a trust level was established when working with strangers. Wariness came as part of grunts' lives.

The Newport Bridge's four-lanes spanned the Saigon River on Highway 1A, the main artery on the northeast side of Saigon. The end of the bridge on the Saigon side was a few blocks from the deepwater docks that unloaded shiploads of war materials. Outbound over the bridge, the highway led directly to the Long Binh - Bien Hoa military complexes. The lifeblood for the flow of logistics ran along it, from docks to depots.

The river itself was about two-hundred meters in width, but each end of the bridge stretched well beyond the river banks and was arched high enough in the center to allow river shipping underneath.

It had been one of the major targets of the Tet offensive, controlling access to Saigon. Fortunately the defending ARVN forces were able to hold their defenseless positions and repel the attack. Another, lone attack took place about four months later, in late May and destroyed two lanes of a span the entire length between two supports. I knew nothing about it at the time, since I was in the field; post Tet activities followed deep into the next few months in our area. Army Engineers made repairs, patching the two lanes with wood timbers, looking out of place like a large scar, but it allowed full use for the constant stream of civilian and military traffic.

Examining each piling beneath the surface of brown, tidal-flow river water was slow business. It was quickly decided that one bridge a day was enough. The team was dropped at their Bien Hoa compound in late afternoons, and we returned the next morning to pick them up. The Major would ask me each morning, "Are you still working on the bridges?" All he wanted to hear was, "Yes sir," and we were gone. I liked the fact that he wasn't some pain in the ass that wanted to know every detail of what I was doing for the day. About all he ever asked was if I had something to do. I always told him yes even when I didn't

Still working in the area a day or two later, I learned the true talent of our guys. They were natural born scroungers. We threw some C-rations in the jeep for lunch, but the Spec 6 team leader said, "We can do better than that. I know where we can get some good, free food. Let's go down and crossover the bridge to the shipping docks."

I still wasn't in full trust of him, but we went, partly out of curiosity to see what he was talking about. We drove down on the docks, and I sat looking around, wondering what in hell we were doing there. It looked vacant of any sign of life when we arrived.

"Okay, just drive real slow along beside these boats," he said as his head moved side to side, scanning each one we passed. A few boats later he said, "Okay, stop here." He jumped out and walked to the edge of the dock where a tugboat was moored. "Hey Captain!" I don't know if he was the captain or not, and neither did he, but it was a good start for chitchat. "You wouldn't happen to have any extra food on there, would you?"

"Yeah, there might be something still in the galley." Seconds later, we were invited aboard and sat down to an unmemorable meal, but it beat C-rations. Afterward, our man smiled. "What did I tell you?"

#

The bridge crossing the Dong Nai River into Bien Hoa was the other one of critical importance, and was duly inspected the same as the Newport. Last on the list that week was a small bridge that spanned one of the feeder tributaries, away from the heavy flow of traffic of the major highway. With much easier access to the water, not far below its underside, we parked on the shoulder of the highway over the bridge.

Those days I wasn't short enough on time left in-country to be overly cautious. I carried only a .45 caliber pistol and a few clips. Rodgers had his M-16 and a bag of magazines, and the floor of our jeep was sandbagged, so we felt safe enough in most areas.

I was glad that I wasn't a diver. It wasn't the image most people had in mind when thinking of the Special Forces. I couldn't understand how they could do more than feel their way around the pilings; it had to be zero visibility in that slow flowing, muddy crap. Since there was a fair amount of natural jetsam floating downstream, I thought it would make good pistol target practice. The diver's safety was never in danger; I watched for challenging targets slowly moving toward the bridge. Coconuts were perfect, and by the time I'd fired every round I had, I was happy with my accuracy. I'd qualified with the .45 back in the States, and didn't particularly like it as a trustworthy weapon, but that day I'd changed my mind. It was re-holstered with satisfaction.

The job ended with that bridge. By then we were one big friendly group, and it was time for a small celebration while the team chief made out his reports. Sitting outside at one of the Bien Hoa bars drinking beer seemed like a good way to spend the remainder of the afternoon. I would've been considerably better off if that was all we had done.

59

A few bottles of beer and the Vietnamese girls who served would no longer come close to our table. I suppose my social graces had not improved to a respectable level. "No - you number ten GI, no more beer," in their well-known descriptive of soldiers they didn't like. I was often a number ten, hardly ever a number one. There were no numbers two through nine that I knew of, although I'd often say, "No, me number five," or three, or eight, but other numbers were never acknowledged.

"I know another place we can go," the team leader said. Since our table was quarantined from service, we picked up and moved onto the next place for a couple more drinks. There was a sign of dusk in the air; time to think about getting on the road back to DiAn.

Whether by design, trying to get my ass in trouble, or simply by not paying attention to the time, which was likely, it got too dark to drive back. I wasn't crazy enough to drive a two-lane road through the boonies back to DiAn after curfew.

"Shit, we're screwed," I said as a general statement of fact. "Do you guys have anything in the way of communications that I can get a message back?" That was a negative. I could visualize the next day when I returned, and not in a good way. My ass was going to be grass.

To not totally write off the night, since what was done was done, the Specialist came up with another idea. "We need a club we can all get in." It wasn't such a simple plan. There were EM clubs for enlisted men, NCO clubs for sergeants, and Officer's clubs with their rank restriction. Our group consisting of a lieutenant, a private, and the other two who were in-between, created a problem.

"Let's drive back over to our compound. I have an idea." One thing I could say about that guy was that he cared even less about rules than I did. We were the only ones in their barrack when we returned. He started going down the lockers, opening each door, since none were locked. A few lockers later, he had pulled out two shirts and berets. After checking the name tags, he said "They're not here now, and won't be needing these. You can wear them."

I thought, 'what the fuck? Is he trying to get me in Leavenworth?' "Are you fucking crazy? Do you know what will happen if we get caught wearing these?" It made no difference; it was the only way we were all going to get into the same club. Rodgers and I instantly became members of the 5th Special Forces.

"Rodgers, you will never open your mouth about tonight - got it." It wasn't a question. "...Or we'll both be up shit creek." We left our shirts, helmets, and his M-16, grabbed the .45 and took off. We drove from Bien Hoa to Long Binh, and parked around back of the largest Enlisted Club in that region of South Vietnam.

Inside the back door on our left was an empty table for four, and a large potted plant that sort of screened it off from the rest of the areas. We sat down, talked and drank. There was really nothing else to do that I could see, so the beers flowed steadily. Every time I finished one, ready to quit, it was "Come on, just one more." I wasn't really a big drinker, and had another four or five beers on top of the afternoon rounds. It was fair to say that I was drunk, but still able to walk what seemed to me to be reasonably straight.

The time came to pee, and the latrine fortunately was a short, direct walk from our table, so there was no weaving around other tables. "I gotta go. Be back in a minute." Nobody else was in there, and as I was leaving I stopped. It was a large room. A row of sinks lined one wall inside the door, and large plate glass mirrors spanned the width of the sinks.

I looked in the mirror, staring. As quick as I could, my fist went through the plate glass with a right jab. Glass shattered. Chards fell in the sinks and bounced on the tile floor, with the attendant noise of glass striking porcelain. Whatever the reason I did that, the mirror held no more images. I was thinking, 'I'm going to be in shit. Maybe I can just pay for the mirror and go' although I couldn't really see that happening, and I didn't have the money anyway.

The first of several who rushed in was a big bastard with a MA armband. MAs served as the keepers of order. He was speechless, couldn't find a word as he looked at me, then the wall where the mirror was then back at me. I said nothing, giving him a shoulder shrug, like 'I don't know what happened.' I think I said, "It just broke." He didn't have time to get any words out of his mouth before my cohorts burst in, close on his heels. They were bug-eyed with a collective 'holy shit' look on their faces.

"It's okay, Sarge. We'll take care of him," not giving the MA time to ask questions. As my new friend grabbed my left arm, blood starting to trickle down my right

We sat down at our table for a couple of minutes. We didn't finish our beers. The team leader said, "It's time to go," while he looked toward the front door. MP's were walking in. He continued, "Slow and quiet" as we slipped out the back door, then picked up speed to the jeep. He looked back as we made our hasty departure; the MP's were still inside - probably finding out what happened.

Rodgers no longer drove. Mr. Quick Thinker was behind the wheel, we were several miles from Bien Hoa, and it was long past travel curfew. We rolled up to one of the closed gates a good distance from the club. "Nobody say anything." It was guarded by MP's, and they weren't about to let us out.

"It's closed for the night." He eyeballed us in the jeep.

I thought 'We're screwed for sure, stuck in Long Binh all night.'

Again, the driver started in with some bullshit story about how critical it was that we get back to Bien Hoa, and how the MP wouldn't be responsible for our safety. I sat in the back and kept my mouth shut. With some hesitation, the MP swung the gate open, "Okay, you're on your own. Good luck."

Our driver turned around and asked for my .45, pulled the slide back to the lock position, and held it in his right hand on the steering wheel while he drove.

It was an eerie ride back, driving through the Vietnamese town of Bien Hoa, without so much as a candle flicker anywhere. The streets and houses were so dark it gave a cleansing effect. We were unable to see the inescapable clouds of dirt that were pervasive during the day. I had no idea where we were, but the two-story houses that lined some of the streets were hulking forms that seemed to close around us as we passed. It wasn't a frightening ride, but still one not to be made more than once.

We were inside the wire at Bien Hoa and stopped when he carefully pulled the slide back on the .45 to release it back to the chamber. I burst out laughing, "You don't have to worry about being careful with that. It doesn't have any bullets in it." I couldn't stop laughing.

It was the first time I'd seen him caught off guard, his feathers ruffled a little. "Goddamnit, you mean we drove back here without any ammo?"

"Yep, I fired every last round at coconuts in the river today."I was still chuckling, "I didn't think it would be a good idea to tell you when we left - didn't want you to be scared."

They took me straight into a bright room with a stainless steel table; I guessed it was their infirmary. I lay on my back while the team leader picked the remaining glass from my hand with some tweezers. That was the last thing I remembered of the night.

My own mind was the one full of ideas after we woke up in the morning. The first thing I told them was, "You're going back with me, and going to help save my ass." We dressed in our correct uniforms, and the four of us got in the jeep, bound for DiAn and Major Taitano.

60

Had we been on the road at the crack of dawn, I could've snuck in before everyone started work, maybe unnoticed as a small ripple on the headquarters pond. 'Hell,' I thought, 'maybe nobody even knew I wasn't there last night.' I was in no condition to move at dawn.

I was always prepared to stand up and take my medicine if I got caught skirting regulations, but in this case I wanted to put the best slant possible on the story.

As we rolled up the blacktop well past daylight, it was time for a briefing: "Keep it simple. We were late finishing the last bridge and got caught by dark by the time we got you back to your quarters. We won't get into any details. You two," speaking to the berets, "are going to do the explaining to the Major. Rodgers will drive me around behind our barracks and let me out so I can clean up with some fresh fatigues and a shave. Just talk to Major Taitano until I get there. you, Rodgers, say nothing at all. Drop them at the office and take off to get cleaned up yourself."

"Leave the Major to us. We know what to do. Everything will be taken care of by the time you get there," the team leader said.

I hoped the smooth talker knew what he was doing. "Okay, just don't fuck me up, or he'll have my ass."

I was confident the plan would go off like clockwork. I was fortunate to live in the back row of rooms so nobody spotted me while I slipped around and quickly got more soldierly looking for the office.

The first person I saw, asked, "Where were you last night? The Chaplain was asking about you?"

'The Chaplain?' Words were difficult to find, unprepared for something like that.

"The Chaplain? Why would he be looking for me? He doesn't even know me." I only saw him in the Officer's Club bar. We were always the first two there. He would be sitting on the same stool, with a highball by the time I arrived. Older and somber for a man of the cloth, we never spoke other than maybe a 'Good afternoon', but usually nothing was said at all. We didn't have a lot in common, except drinking time, and I always sat a few seats down the bar. I was sure he was Catholic although the chaplains were usually nondenominational in nature.

"I don't know. Somebody came in yesterday afternoon and said they saw your jeep on one of the bridges, but never saw you back last night."

'Why the fuck can't people mind their own business? Damn, if the Chaplain was asking around about me, everybody was going to know. Shit, this can't get any worse.' At brigade headquarters, the bar was the only place to be every night, and it always had a crowd because headquarters was about ninety-percent officers. There was a small theater room showing a movie, the bar itself, and a poker game at one of the tables. I was there every night, normally.

It was looking bleaker by the second with nothing to do but see if the berets were having any luck. Maybe there would be no more than an ass-chewing, and it would stop there. I didn't want to get on Colonel Gallagher's list too.

The berets were sitting in Major Taitano's partitioned-off, but not sound proof office. Without an expression I walked in, ready for what was to come. It was like a fucking party, talking and laughing - one big happy family. Without a word of rebuke from the major, I wasn't about to raise any concern or questions. I told him I needed to get them back to Bien Hoa.

They had done their job better than I ever expected. "What in hell did you tell him, for him to be smiling? He didn't give a shit about the whole thing."

"He spent five years in the 5th Special Forces; we were just talking about his days in the 5th. He's a good guy. We both told him you did a good job with us; we would work with you anytime."

61

"I have another job for you." I don't know that Lieutenant Colonel Gallagher ever called me by my name more than a handful of times; he usually just started right in with whatever plans he had. "This is a big one; Division wants us to get involved with security for the bridges going into Saigon and Bien Hoa. We're going to furnish them with concussion grenades for guards to toss in the river during the night. Five thousand have been ordered, but won't be in country for a while. Do you think you can make up something for them to use in the meantime? Can you do explosives?"

"Yes sir, I can handle it."

"Good. Head down to the Bien Hoa ammo dump and get everything you need. Let me know how it comes out.

This was an extension of the operation performed by the Special Forces dive team. After they confirmed the underwater defensive fortifications, the special grenades were to provide an extra layer of defense.

Private Rodgers and I made the trip to requisition the needed supplies of several cases of half-pound explosive blocks, time fuse, blasting caps, and pull-ring fuse starters.

We pulled under a small shade tree between the S-5 and S-3 buildings and laid out the materials across the back of the jeep to begin assembly. We set out cutting the time fuse to burn a safe length of about ten seconds before detonation, inserting one end in the pull starter and the other in a blasting cap. The fuse assembly could then be pushed into the block of explosive. Our only tool was an old pair of lineman wire pliers we found to do the fuse-cutting and crimping of the caps.

We'd worked our way into a good unhurried rhythm of cutting, poking, and crimping, before being interrupted.

"What've you guys been doing out here?" Out of curiosity, someone strolled from the Operations building we happened to be parked beside.

The small wooden boxes stacked on the jeep should have been giveaways. About anything delivered in wood boxes was meant to go BOOM! Ours were filled with half-pound blocks of an equivalent to TNT.

"We're making up some concussion grenades," I said, proud of our work, and went back about my business.

A few minutes later a higher rank came out to tell us, "You've got to move away from here," meaning from beside the operations building.

"What a bunch of whiney-ass REMF's. Come on Rodgers, let's find another spot."

We filled several boxes and made a run down to the bridge that crossed to the Bien Hoa, Long Binh areas. A permanent ARVN unit lived on the river bank far below the pavement.

I decided we had better toss the first one in shallow water near the edge in case it was not waterproof for long when submerged - maybe not waterproof at all. There was a slight skepticism on my part as to the effectiveness. I was wrong. It made the sound of a muffled bass drum then blew a ten-foot plume of water straight up.

"Damn. Wha-hoo, that worked, didn't it? I think we'd better toss the next one in deeper water."

Our test successful, we left the homemade batch of grenades at the bridge, with instructions.

"Don't use these for fishing, and don't use them all in one night. Just throw one out near the bridge supports every few hours but not at regular intervals. Understand?"

Promises were made for judicious use of the grenades.

Their next delivery was a jeep full of raw materials. We laid out the components, showed them how to make one or two, gave them a test, and said good luck. It gave them something to do during the day as they sat around. Again, promises were made to make them last until the shipment of the proper grenades arrived.

#

The arrival of five thousand grenades brought new problems. There were hundreds of wooden cases that needed transport and storage. I didn't want to leave them at the Long Binh ammo dump in fear they would be poached if someone else found they were there, and I couldn't leave that many at the bridges where they would go, thinking they would be used too fast.

The only logical solution was to transport them to our own ammo storage facility at DiAn where I could regularly draw small amounts for distribution. Rodgers picked up a two-and-a-half ton truck at the motor pool for our first load.

It was late in the day, about closing time when we got to DiAn with the load of grenades. We went straight to our ammo dump. It looked like we were going to miss chow time by the time we unloaded and stacked our goods. It got worse when the sergeant in charge of storage refused our entry in no certain terms. We weren't going to put anything in there, claiming it was full.

265

I knew I couldn't leave a truck full of explosives parked out in the open all night. It was time to visit Lieutenant-Colonel Gallagher for a solution. We went back to brigade headquarters, and I went straight to the colonel's office only to find him gone. The Brigade Executive Officer's office was next door and he asked me what I wanted. The XO was an academic-looking Lieutenant-Colonel, who wore yellow sunglasses all the time. I'd never been around him much, but explained my predicament, expecting no help.

"Come with me." He took off to the next building over. We headed directly to the office of the major who had jurisdiction over all supply matters, including the ammo facility. The major was leaning back, feet on his desk, twirling a tennis racket when we entered.

'A tennis racket?' I thought. 'Where in hell are there tennis courts around here?' I was focused with jaw-dropping disbelief that anybody had that little to do for a job. 'What a REMF this guy is.'

The colonel wasn't amused at all. "Lock your heels together when I walk in the room, Major!" He flew out of his chair and stood at attention. It didn't take long for the major to understand that there would be room to store what I needed at the ammo dump. The colonel spun around and left at the same speed he entered, and I was right on his heels fearing some kind of retribution for being a troublemaker from the major.

By the time I got back to the ammo dump, we were welcomed to store our load and never had any more trouble when we pulled up for any reason.

62

By November, the wet season rains tapered to an end, returning to the suffocating heat of the dry season. I arrived in the dry season and knew by the time the next dry season came around I would be close to going home. I wasn't a true short-timer yet, but I was feeling good and enjoying my job for the time I had left.

The canvas top came off the jeep, and the windshield was hinged forward to rest on the hood. It gave a convenient place on which to rest the barrel of my rifle. It may not sound like much, but the top and windshield in the up positions blocked free movement for weapons if I ever needed to fire.

My Colt .45 caliber pistol was put away. With my time getting shorter, I decided it was time to upgrade our security on the roads. I scrounged an M-14E2, the modified version of the standard M-14. It had a pistol grip stock, a fold down front hand grip, and folding bi-pods on the underside of the front sight. It was the hardcore weapon of choice in the field; it was heavy as hell, but that was no longer a consideration. With a bag of magazines, I felt as safe as possible. It was a fearsome weapon, and I carried it until I quit going outside the wire. The jeep's floor was layered with full sandbags, edge-to-edge tight. Along with my steel pot, it was as much insurance as I could supply, trusting that dumb luck would keep its distance.

On the days without a specific job to do, we rode around checking the pin locations from my office map. If we found an installation, I checked their fortifications to see if there was anything I could do to easily improve their defensive positions. Usually additional sandbags or concertina wire were the most I could offer. Some days we rode around to no place special, simply looking around the countryside.

One of our excursions took us up a dirt road obviously designed and made by engineers. We had passed by it a number of times and I was curious about where it went. It rose to a distant, low-lying hilltop covered with trees, then disappeared.

Near the dark, shaded canopy of the trees, an American soldier walked out. "Westbrook! What in the hell are you doing around here?" It was a classmate from Fort Benning. He'd walked out when he saw a jeep coming up the road. Before attending Officer Candidate School, he was a sergeant with one tour in Vietnam under his belt. I didn't know him very well at Benning since we were in separate platoons.

We shook hands with the mutual "Good to see you again."

"I'm with MAC-V, an advisor with the ARVN unit up here." His clothes were laundered and neat, befitting the reputation of MAC-V advisors. They were known to be one of the easiest assignments in the field.

"What? Couldn't the Army find you a real job? How'd you get a job like that anyway?"

He laughed at my sarcasm about his cushy assignment and asked what I was doing out riding around. We talked a few minutes about our jobs, other classmates we had news about, and time left in country. It was a brief visit before we wished each other well.

"Take care of yourself."

"Hey, you too,"

#

"What the fuck was that?" I yelled to Rodgers, above the wind and engine noise. "You think somebody was shooting at us?" It was pretty much a rhetorical question since we were driving about forty-five mph. It was a single shot, enough to make my stomach go to my throat in the micro-second before I could react.

He shrugged, "I don't know." It didn't hit anything, and we were well past the spot by the time we had to think about it.

"Yeah, probably some little ARVN bastard sitting there thinking it was fun."

It happened again, different road, different day. After the same initial reaction as before, of momentarily scaring the shit out of me, it pissed me off. I looked for a place we could get the jeep off the highway, ready to circle back through the bush and teach the son of a bitch what a real surprise was like. A quick second thought and I decided it wasn't a smart thing to do.

#

The colonel came looking for me one morning. It was well past work time, but I didn't know because I was still in my bunk. I'd not quite recovered from a late night of drinking and poker. He sent one of the clerks to find me and let me know he was waiting. Otherwise, it was a normal morning, and he didn't mention my lateness. I thought, 'Good, I survived that. He wasn't upset at all."

Surfer Joe had gone to Division Headquarters the afternoon before on an overnight trip, so I felt no rush to work that morning. However, he was there when I got in that afternoon and called me into his flimsily partitioned office from where everyone in the building heard what was said.

269

"You were late this morning." The major wasn't asking a question. He was stating a fact in his calm conversational style of speaking. "I heard the colonel came over looking for you, and you weren't here."

'Damn. How does he find out about these things?' My mind was trying to anticipate the next step. 'Probably going to be an ass-chewing. Colonel Gallagher must have told him, and here it comes down the line.' I knew nobody in the offices said anything.

"Yes sir." What else was I going to say; he wasn't the type who bought bullshit, and I wasn't about to offer any.

"Why not?"

"Too late drinking, sir. I didn't hear my alarm this morning." Drinking and poker were my nightly staples of self amusement.

"Don't let it happen again." He spoke still with a calm voice, as if he wasn't concerned in the least, but with an understanding it would not be so quiet if it happened again.

"No sir, it won't."

'That was it? Don't do it again? I dodged a bullet on that one.' My mind was in a state of unbelievable relief after expecting a hail of wrath. 'Maybe he had to say something to me, because the colonel told him I was late, then told him to take care of it, properly using the chain of command.' I was still thinking, although the incident was over. Getting called to the office was an embarrassment if nothing else, but I was prepared to stand up for my decisions or actions.

Bruce, the lieutenant in charge of PsyOps said, "I'm a few minutes late every morning, ten or fifteen minutes, but guess it's okay. He's never said anything about it." I didn't know if it was his way to console me, or if he was being smug about the latitude in tardiness he received. I cared less; his ten minutes didn't compare to my screw up on the matter of lateness.

"Yeah? Well, there is no doubt in my military mind whatsoever that I will not be late again," Despite what I told the major, I knew timeliness was going to be a problem. I was a sound sleeper and seldom woke up when the sirens started because of mortars or rockets coming in on the airstrip. I knew I would not have to worry about it immediately, though. I had a plan.

For the next two nights, I left the club early and walked back to the office where I pushed two of the large, gray, metal desks together. I slept on top, thinking nothing of it except I didn't want to be seen. The desks were no more uncomfortable than the many nights I spent on ambushes.

My habits changed. I stopped the poker. A small group of us moved to one of the larger quarters and played Hearts and Spades; no more gambling. Booze was left at the club. Nights became fun.

#

Somewhere along the way, Major Taitano seemed more like a friend, as much as the separate ranks allowed. Maybe it was because of my short stint with the Special Forces team; I never knew exactly what they told him. Possibly it was the fact that I took care of everything Colonel Gallagher needed, without problems. We both played in after-work volleyball games, where very few rules applied; there was lots of body contact at the net. The games were when the tag 'Surfer Joe' was given to the major. He would have me drive him places when I was sitting around the office doing nothing. He showed me pictures of his wife in his office, as I did the same for him earlier with the photos on my desk. We talked about Hawaii, his home, after I told him about R&R there. He knew Don Ho, had gone to school with him, but felt fame had changed him for the worse.

One afternoon he called. "Lieutenant Park, come here. Look at this." He was holding a newly published magazine. I think it was *Screw*. As new competition for *Playboy*, I thought it was going to be a nude picture. He opened the centerfold vertically and flipped it around for me, then burst out laughing.

271

It was a petition. In huge red letters across the top, it read
FUCK THE WAR. My mouth dropped open, horrified but
speechless, unsure how to react to his laughter. There were two
pages of lines for signatures below the heading. I saw no
humor, but managed a courtesy smile that no way compared to
the humor he took from it. Our contrast in reaction showed me
the seriousness I had taken in life; I still had the inflexibility of
believing in the political morality of the war and took issue
with anything that protested its righteousness.

"A friend of mine sent this to me, just for this page." He
was referring to the petition. "He thinks I'm crazy for being
over here." Surfer Joe was still chuckling.

The major knew the intent of his friend to get a rise out of
him, and he couldn't take it seriously; it was an inside joke
between two friends. I was shocked at his reaction, unable to
understand a career officer laughing about our war. I was a
draftee going home and would be a civilian in a few months. I
should have been the one doing the laughing. I guess in reality
it showed how far removed we were from the real war,
working at a large headquarters unit, but I was still close to my
platoon leader ideals.

#

The boss called Bruce to his office one morning. He was
the lieutenant in charge of the PsyOps part of our offices in S-
5. He was a good enough guy; we talked every now and then,
but had no friendship outside the office.

He confided one day that he had been relieved from his job
as platoon leader in the field. A battalion staff officer in a
helicopter had spotted him; caught him using one of the
beaten-down paths that served as a road. Patrols never used
roads, paths, or trails; it was in the SOP, and meant an
automatic relief of command. No defense or explanations were
accepted.

"It's not like we were using the road for patrol. It was going the same direction we were at the moment, and tactically it wouldn't have made any difference if we were walking ten feet to one side of it."

I didn't doubt his story. He was seen in the wrong place, if there even for a short distance. Rules were rules.

"Shit, they could have relieved me a dozen times for shit like that. They just never caught me. Hell, we had this dumb-ass company commander who must have thought the roads were put there for us to walk on. I wish somebody had seen him so we could've kissed his ass goodbye - the sorry bastard."

#

Bruce was seriously mistaken about Major Taitano not noticing his constant morning tardiness. It was several weeks after my mistake of being late, but I was on time all other mornings. I don't know what brought it on that morning, but the major called Bruce into his office, and I was pretty sure the ass-chewing could be heard a building or two away. At a level of anger I didn't know existed within the major, he made it clear that Bruce would never be late to the office again.

In less than a minute, I was quietly easing toward the door where my jeep was parked, afraid to even be seen by the major that morning and wanting out before he finished. I felt embarrassed for Bruce.

"Come on, Rodgers. Jesus, Major Taitano is on the fucking warpath this morning, and we're not going to hang around to find out what's next. Let's find someplace to be."

63

I went about my business of helping wherever I could. I delivered a few rolls of concertina wire, sandbags, or an occasional small generator with powerful floodlights to the smaller outposts. At times there was nothing in particular to do; I learned to become inconspicuous during the day, out of sight somewhere in the jeep. Sometimes I rode around in Saigon, careful to not be seen by anyone of importance.

Big jobs were all completed, and everything else was under control. I was appreciative of the unexpected praise when Colonel Gallagher awarded me a Bronze Star medal for meritorious service as I neared my time to go home. It was always a pleasure working for him, as well as Surfer Joe.

#

Like other moves or job changes I experienced in Vietnam, the end came without advance notice. Two or three weeks before I was scheduled to leave, my replacement arrived. I walked into work one day and there he stood. I extended the same courtesy to him as I had received. We made the rounds to district headquarters. I briefed him about the pins on the office map and what the different colors meant. He didn't care, stating he would develop his own system, with a hint of superiority. I wished him luck.

Once the transition was made, I had no need to go outside the wire on a daily basis. Nobody questioned my disappearance from the office. As long as someone was there to fill the job, Surfer Joe left me to my own desires. Befitting my status of deadweight, my days were spent sleeping in and sunbathing beside my room during the best hours of the day. The least I could do was arrive home in the dead of winter with a suntan. A true short-timer at last, I got my orders to ship out and had nothing to do but wait.

Sitting in the office's club one night, one of the lieutenants was talking loudly to the point of boasting about how he knew the sergeant at 90th Replacement Company who was in charge of all outgoing personnel. He was assured of leaving at the earliest date when his time came.

As I got within a few days of my time to leave, I decided to make a trip down to the 90th to see if I could find this sergeant and do a little name dropping, to see what might happen. Sure enough, he could get me out on the next day's flight. Rodgers and I made a fast run back to DiAn to grab my belongings, which were already laid out and get back to Long Binh that afternoon.

I went by the office to tell the major and guys goodbye. Major Taitano was out of the office so I missed him, but knew he would understand when Rodgers told him I needed to get to Long Binh. I was three days ahead of schedule, and all I could think about was home.

That night in the officer's club at the 90th Replacement, I ran into another classmate on his way home, along with another departing lieutenant. The three of us depleted the club's inventory of seven bottles of champagne. Our behavior was in line with our alcohol consumption and luckily we were never asked to hold it down. The next day I was homeward bound.

#

The plane load of soldiers was absolutely silent. It was midday as we prepared to taxi down the runway. Even in this relative safety, a level of apprehension still existed. The captain's voice came over the intercom. "Let's see if we can get this big mother off the ground." It brought a round of laughter and cheers. Only when the wheels lifted off the tarmac, and we had climbed to what I was sure was beyond range of ground fire did I exhale in complete relief.

Ten thousand miles later, it was near dark and pouring rain when we landed in Oakland, California. I went through the exit procedures quickly. As I stepped outside the terminal to breathe the fresh air, a captain asked if I wanted to share a cab to the San Francisco Airport. We left the gathering herd of soldiers milling around, eager to get our names on standby flights to home before the airport filled with soldiers, all wanting flights. I wanted any flights going east and was lucky to get on the list for a flight to Atlanta.

The San Francisco airport was like a refrigerator in January, and night time had turned it into a ghost town. I sat in a short-sleeve khaki uniform attempting to look comfortable. The captain and I both got our names on our desired flights; there was nothing to do but sit in a dimly lit bar with a drink, and wait.

I didn't call home. It was already late at night, and I was unsure if I would be on the flight to Atlanta until the last minute. I wanted my surprise arrival time to be assured and didn't call until I got to Atlanta, a one hour flight from Nashville. It was six o'clock in the morning on January 23.

A Christmas tree was still up when I got home, but being home was the greatest gift.

THE END

Military Abbreviations Used In This Book

AO – Area of Operation
APC – Armored Personnel Carriers)
ARVN – South Vietnamese Army
Chicom – Chinese communist
CO – Commanding Officer
CP – Command Post
KIA – Killed In Action
LAW – Light Antitank Weapon
LOH – Light Observation Helicopter
LP – Listening Post
LRRP – Long Range Reconnaissance Patrol
LZ – Landing Zone
MIA – Missing in Action
MP – Military Police
NDP – Night Defensive Position
NVA – North Vietnamese Army
OCS – Officer Candidate School
OD – Olive Drab
POW – Prisoner of War
PX – Post Exchange
PZ – Pickup Zone
REMF – Rear Echelon Mother Fucker
ROTC – Reserve Officer Training Corp
RPG – Rocket Propelled Grenade
R&R – Rest and Relaxation
RRF – Ready Reserve Force
RTO – Radio Operator
Sit-Rep – Situation Report
VC – Viet Cong
WIA – Wounded in Action
XO -- Executive Officer

ABOUT THE AUTHOR

Steve Park served in the US Army during the height of the Vietnam War. As an Infantry Platoon Leader (Lieutenant), turning back the enemy, while ensuring the safety of his men, was his highest priority. The writing of BOOTS was both therapeutic and a means to provide an accurate account of what it was like to serve in a combat role. Steve is an accomplished artist and lives with Sherry, his wife of 46 years, in Lake Wylie, South Carolina. They share their home with three rescue dogs. BOOTS is his first book.

23713822R00153

Made in the USA
Lexington, KY
20 June 2013